THE LONDON
MARKET GUIDE

Andrew Kershman

The London Market Guide

Written by Andrew Kershman
Additional research and writing by
Catherine Belonogoff
Cover photographs by Metro
Photography by Andrew Kershman
Edited by Abigail Willis
Maps by Lesley Gilmour
Design by Metro

Published in 2004 by
Metro Publications
PO Box 6336
London
N1 6PY

Printed and bound in India by Thomson Press Ltd

© 2004 Andrew Kershman

British Library Cataloguing in Publication Data.
A catalogue record for this book is available from the British Library.

ISBN   1 902910 14 1

Berwick Street Market

ACKNOWLEDGEMENTS

My thanks go to all the stall holders who patiently answered my questions and even agreed to pose for a photograph. My editor, Abigail Willis, deserves special praise for her efforts particularly towards the end, when last minute changes and corrections where made. Lesley Gilmour also merits a special mention for her sterling work on the maps and illustrations for the book. My thanks also go to Susi Koch whose support and hard work have helped make this book possible.

CONTENTS

Introduction 1
Market Map 2-3

CENTRAL LONDON
Berwick Street & Rupert Street 6
Charing Cross Collectors' Fair 9
The Courtyard 12
Covent Garden 14
Earlham Street 18
Leadenhall 20
Leather Lane 22
Lower Marsh 26
Piccadilly Market 30
Smithfield 34
South Bank Book Market 36
Strutton Ground 39
Tachbrook Street 42
Whitecross Street 44

NORTH LONDON
Alfie's Antiques Market 48
Bell Street 51
Camden 54
Camden Passage 62
Chalton Street 66
Chapel Market 69
Church Street 71
Hampstead Community Market 75
Hoxton Street 77
Inverness Street 80
Kilburn Square 82
Nag's Head 84
Queen's Crescent 86
Swiss Cottage 88
Wembley Sunday Market 92

WEST LONDON
Bayswater Road & Piccadilly 96
Hammersmith Road 99
King's Road Antiques 101
North End Road 103
Portobello 106
Shepherd's Bush 116

SOUTHWEST LONDON
Battersea High Street 120
Brixton Market 122
Broadway and Tooting 127
Hildreth Street 130
Merton Abbey Mills 132
Nine Elms Sunday Market 136
Northcote Road 138
Wimbledon Stadium 142

SOUTHEAST LONDON
Bermondsey 146
Borough Market 150
Choumert Road & Rye Lane 154
Deptford Market 157
East Street 160
Elephant & Castle 164
Greenwich Market 166
Lewisham High Street 173
Southwark Park Road 174
Westmoreland Road 176
Woolwich & Plumstead Road 178

EAST LONDON
Bethnal Green Road 182
Billingsgate 186
Brick Lane 188
Chrisp Street 195
Columbia Road 197
Kingsland Waste 200
Petticoat Lane 204
Queen's Market 210
Ridley Road 212
Roman Road 216
Spitalfields 220
Walthamstow 224
Well Street 228
Whitechapel 229

Farmers' Markets 232
Car Boot Sales 237
Top Twelve London Markets 239
The Week at a Glance 240
Appendix 242
Index 244

Columbia Road Market

INTRODUCTION

Visiting the street markets of London in the course of researching this new edition has again been a memorable experience. Particular conversations, the cries of traders at the close of the market as they try to clear their stock, or the discovery of an unusual gem in a box of junk, all these things have made an impression. When was the last time you had a memorable experience in the provisions aisle of your local supermarket?

There have been a lot of changes in London's market scene in the last two years and many of them have been positive improvements. It has been particularly heartening to witness the huge expansion in the number of Farmers' Markets in the capital. These markets have become a valuable lifeline for struggling local farmers enabling them to sell their produce direct to the public and also share some of their enthusiasm for food with their customers. Visiting Pimlico Farmers' Market recently I was able to buy delicious varieties of honey for just a few pounds and talk with the farmer about his hives. Likewise, the farm producing fresh apple juice for £3 a bottle, did not sell a generic apple juice but instead a variety of pressings with very different flavours. This guide now has a section dedicated to farmers' markets. There are also other foodie markets in the capital, with Borough weekend food market growing in popularity, and Merton Abbey Mills now offering a selection of quality food stalls.

Not all the changes of the last few years have been good news. Flea markets have suffered recently with Bell Street and the second-hand section of Brixton Market dwindling to just a few stalls. At both markets traders complained about the high rents charged by the local council and the increased use of regulations to hinder their ability to trade. My recent discovery of Deptford Market with its vibrant junk and bric-à-brac yard on Douglas Street shows that such markets can thrive with the support of the local community and a more tolerant approach from the council.

It would be easy to blame councils for the difficulties that some markets face these days, but in many cases there are other reasons. Roman Road in the East End has a good local market that is losing out to nearby supermarkets and out of town shopping centres. The dispirited traders from markets like Roman Road could get some inspiration from a visit to Northcote Road, where the market has adapted to changes in the area and now offers a more varied and distinctive selection of fine food, clothes, toys and flowers, as well as market essentials like fruit and veg. One fashion trader had decorated her wagon, made business cards and created something closer to a pavement boutique than a conventional stall. This kind of approach might not work in poorer parts of town, but it is still good to see traders re-thinking what can be done with a market stall.

At the time of writing Brick Lane is in a state of flux with a major building development affecting the location of the bric-à-brac stalls from week to week. Markets – particularly in an ever-evolving city like London – are susceptible to this sort of disruption and although I have taken a lot of trouble to ensure the accuracy of each entry some discrepancies are inevitable. Nothing stays the same and this constant change is part of what makes London's markets interesting and vibrant places to explore.

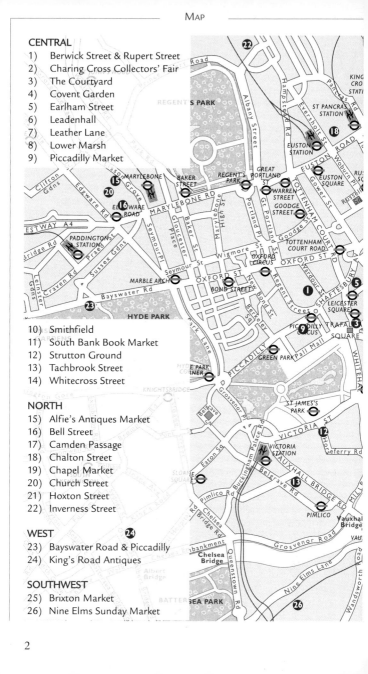

CENTRAL

1) Berwick Street & Rupert Street
2) Charing Cross Collectors' Fair
3) The Courtyard
4) Covent Garden
5) Earlham Street
6) Leadenhall
7) Leather Lane
8) Lower Marsh
9) Piccadilly Market

10) Smithfield
11) South Bank Book Market
12) Strutton Ground
13) Tachbrook Street
14) Whitecross Street

NORTH

15) Alfie's Antiques Market
16) Bell Street
17) Camden Passage
18) Chalton Street
19) Chapel Market
20) Church Street
21) Hoxton Street
22) Inverness Street

WEST

23) Bayswater Road & Piccadilly
24) King's Road Antiques

SOUTHWEST

25) Brixton Market
26) Nine Elms Sunday Market

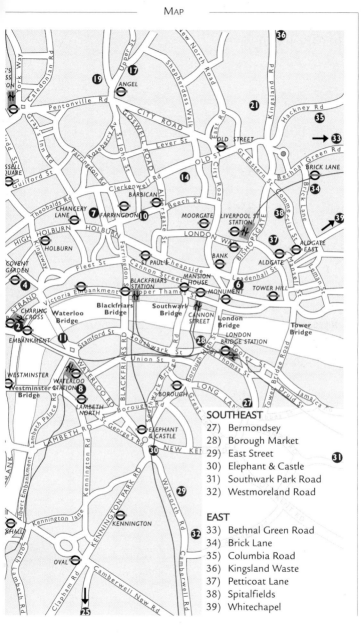

SOUTHEAST

27) Bermondsey
28) Borough Market
29) East Street
30) Elephant & Castle
31) Southwark Park Road
32) Westmoreland Road

EAST

33) Bethnal Green Road
34) Brick Lane
35) Columbia Road
36) Kingsland Waste
37) Petticoat Lane
38) Spitalfields
39) Whitechapel

central

ICON INDEX

 antiques

 books

 fruit & veg

 cut flower & plants

 cloth

 fresh fish

 towels & bedding

 fresh bread

 pubs

fresh coffee

produce

hardware

arts & crafts

clothing

shoes

household goods

fresh meat

furniture

cafés & restaurants

bric-a-brac

music (CD's etc)

electrical goods

toys

toiletries

pet supplies

haberdashery

CENTRAL LONDON

Berwick Street & Rupert Street 6
Charing Cross Collectors' Fair 9
The Courtyard 12
Covent Garden 14
Earlham Street 18
Leadenhall 20
Leather Lane 22
Lower Marsh 26
Piccadilly Market 30
Smithfield 34
South Bank Book Market 36
Strutton Ground 39
Tachbrook Street 42
Whitecross Street 44

BERWICK STREET & RUPERT STREET, W1

Berwick St, from Broadwick St extending south onto Rupert St
Tube: Oxford Circus (Victoria, Central), Piccadilly Circus (Bakerloo, Piccadilly), Tottenham Court Road (Northern)
Bus: 38, 19, 14 (Shaftesbury Avenue)
7, 8 10, 25, 55, 73, 98, 176 (Oxford Street)
Open: Monday-Saturday 9am-5pm

Berwick Street is one of those special places that seem to capture something of the flavour of London and its people. There's been a fruit and veg market here since the 1840's and although there are some signs of modernity such as the supermarket and tower block at the junction with Peter Street, the street and market still exude much of their old character.

Berwick Street market is a one-off because it is essentially a local market dealing in fruit and veg, but situated bang in the heart of

London's Soho. Despite being restricted to the west side of the street and a gradual decline in the number of stalls, Berwick Street is still a wonderful fruit and veg market with just about every fruit, vegetable and herb you could possibly need from the humble potato to Chinese black mushrooms and cassava. If you're looking for a particular delicacy the traders are always willing to point you to the right stall. More basic fruit and veg is often sold very cheaply with large bags of bananas, oranges or mushrooms going for £1, although it is a sensible idea to check the quality of the goods before buying. The produce is still very good, but the elaborate displays of fruit and veg that were once a feature of the Peter Street end of the market are a thing of the past.

Supplementing the fruit and veg stalls is the long-established and excellent fish stall offering fresh fish collected that day from Billingsgate. Ronnie's flower stall is still going strong and makes a colourful display in the centre of Berwick Street. The stalls selling fine cheeses and bread have both now disappeared, which is indicative of the market's gradual decline. In their place are a number of stalls offering household and small electrical goods as well as a very well organised CD, DVD and video stall.

By walking south across Peter Street and through the narrow pedestrian Walker's Court (with porno outlets on either side), Rupert Street market can be reached. This market used to have some fruit and veg stalls, but they have gone in the last few years leaving a handful of stalls selling bags, belts and cheap new clothing. Amid all the combat clothing and novelty T-shirts there were one or two interesting things such as leather belts for £7.99, but generally speaking Rupert Street is now a very small and run-down market. The main attraction here is Cheapo Cheapo Records (53 Rupert Street) which is one of London's best discount music shops and well worth a visit.

Anyone who loves London's markets must harbour some resentment towards Westminster Council for the changes in recent years, but the development of inner city supermarkets has also taken its toll on the market, and traders now claim the congestion charge is making matters even worse.

Refreshment

The number and variety of eating places on Berwick Street has greatly increased in recent years. Bar Du Marché and The Mediterranean Café are both at the northern end of Berwick Street, as is the trendy Beatroot vegetarian café. There is also a long established fish and chip restaurant at the Broadwick Street end of the market. For those wanting a pint in a traditional dingy British pub the King of Corsica on Berwick Street will not disappoint.

Local Attractions

Berwick Street is also a good place to look for fabric sold by the metre with lots of shops including Borovick Fabric and Soho Silks. For those interested in cutting edge music, there are also numerous trendy vinyl stores along Berwick Street, but these are not places to visit if you are looking for the latest Robbie Williams' LP, although Rough Trade is a little more mainstream.

Getting a Stall

For further details about a stall at either Berwick or Rupert Street contact Westminster City Council (see appendix).

CHARING CROSS COLLECTORS' FAIR, WC2

Under Charing Cross Arches (end of Northumberland Avenue)

Tube: Embankment (Northern, Bakerloo, District and Circle)
Charing Cross (Northern, Jubilee and Bakerloo)

Rail: *Charing Cross*

Bus: *6, 9, 11, 13, 15, 23, 77A, 91, 176 (Strand);*
24, 29 (Charing Cross Road); 3, 12, 53, 77A, 88, 159, 453 (Whitehall)

Open: *Saturday 8.30am-1pm*

Every Saturday, hundreds of collectors congregate in an unprepossessing underground car park in central London. Displayed on the fifty or so stalls are military medals, coins, stamps, bank notes, postcards, cigarette cards and even phone cards. Collecting things can seem to the uninitiated a dull, rather unexciting pastime and the initial impression when entering this concrete bunker will probably confirm this view. The average age of those attending is about fifty, they are nearly all male and a very great number sport beards of some description often in conjunction with a cardigan of grey or brown hue. If you can resist the temptation to run, a brief wander among the stalls is sure to unearth something of interest. The coins on display are a good first stop because of their intrinsic appeal. The neatly written labels give details of the type and age of the coin and the dealer is usually willing to expound at length if you want to know more. I was surprised that some coins of considerable antiquity were so cheap. An English half groat dating from 1461 could be bought here for £16, a Roman denarius for £23 and a Syrian coin from 142 BC for only £12. Other coins of various denominations and ages were piled in great heaps for only a few pence each. It is here that I discovered that my only family heirloom (a 1965 coin commemorating Winston Churchill) was worth the princely sum of 60p.

There are many stamp dealers here selling all kinds of stamps. It is possible to start a collection for only a few pence but in some instances whole collections are for sale. I asked one bearded, cardigan-clad stall-holder the value of his most expensive stamp, but my question was clearly a crass one for his brow creased and he explained that he didn't think about his collection in that way and then generously volunteered the figure of £75 to help me.

The postcard stalls are a little more accessible to the first-time visitor. They are usually arranged by country or area, but in some cases by subject and are fascinating not only for the aging pictures on the front but often for the handwritten messages found on the back, addressed to long deceased correspondents. The political postcards are interesting, one card commemorated the Locarno Conference of 1925 with pictures of the participants including a young Mussolini, while another French postcard used a cartoon to lambaste Prussian Imperialism. Although not a collector I was tempted by the notion of owning a little bit of history for only a few pounds.

I meandered through the rest of the fair unmoved by the large collection of phone cards and positively revolted by the idea of possessing war medals that had originally belonged to men who had paid a good deal more than a few pounds for them. I departed with only a large and shiny dollar coin as a souvenir of my visit and to add to my now much devalued heirloom.

Refreshment

The Collectors' Fair is located in the centre of town and is surrounded by cafés, restaurants and pubs. The Café in the Crypt, below St Martins-in-the-Fields church on Trafalgar Square, is just 5 minutes away and is a quirky original among a sea of coffee chains.

Local Attractions

There are many places to visit after a morning at the Collectors' Fair, including The National Portrait Gallery, The National Gallery and The Photographers' Gallery. Just accross the river is The South Bank Centre which always has a busy programme of events and concerts and also features a great book market under Waterloo Bridge (see page 36).

Getting a Stall

For further details contact the market manager on 01483 281 771.

THE COURTYARD, WC2

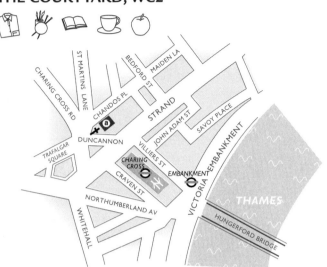

St Martin-in-the-Fields Church Courtyard, Trafalgar Square WC2
Tube/Rail: *Charing Cross*
Bus: *6, 9, 11, 13, 15, 23, 77A, 91, 176 (Strand);*
24, 29 (Charing Cross Road)
Open: *Daily 10am-7pm*

There's been a church on this central London site for nearly a thousand years – although the present edifice is the work of James Gibbs and dates from 1724. The market that sets up in the Church's courtyard is a much more recent development, having been established in the early 1980's. The stalls are very largely geared to cater for the many tourists that visit the area and the Trafalgar Square end of the market is awash with Union Jacks, T-shirts with pictures of red buses on them and Beefeater dolls. Further into the market many other nationalities are represented, there are jumpers from Peru, ornaments of Hindu deities, Egyptian-style paintings and models of pharoahs, African masks and silk dresses from China. It is inexplicable why a market in the centre of London aimed at tourists should sell so many souvenirs of other countries – do visting French tourists return home with a realistic plastic model of Tutankhamun saying "look what I've brought back from London". Or for that matter, do you find models of the Tower of London in Paris markets?

It's both easy and enjoyable to criticise this market, but among the thirty or so stalls I did manage to find one or two interesting things. The Chinese traders had some attractive silk tops for £20 and the leather stall at the back of the market offered a good range of leather gear, including fashionable motorcycle jackets for only £70. The book stall is worth a visit with its small but good quality mix of mint condition literature for about half the retail price. There is even a small fruit and veg stall offering a few essentials among the tye-dye T-shirts, scented soap and strange smoking devices that surround it. The Courtyard is also an attractive place to visit with ancient stone paving, trees providing shade in the summer and wrought iron railings.

Refreshment

The Crypt Café (entrance on Duncannon Street) is located in the church's basement, and is a large and pleasant space serving wholesome food and good coffee. If you prefer to remain above ground, there is an Aroma Café just a minute away at the bottom of St Martin's Lane.

Local Attractions

St Martin-in-the-Field Church offers regular classical music recitals, many of them during the lunch hour. The market is also just opposite The National Portrait Gallery and National Gallery for those wanting a bit of culture after their shopping.

Getting Stall

For further details contact the market manager on 0794 991 4411 or contact the head office of the market organisers (Waterman Associates) on 020 7930 7821.

COVENT GARDEN, W2

a) Jubilee Marke
b) Apple Market

Covent Garden Piazza

Tube: Covent Garden (Piccadilly)

Bus: 6, 9, 11, 13, 15, 23, 77A, 91, 139, 176 (Strand);
14, 19, 24, 29, 38 (Charing Cross Road)

Open: Monday 10:30am-7:30pm (antiques), Tuesday-Sunday 10:30am-
7:30pm (arts & crafts market); every 2nd Friday of the month 10am-7pm
(food lover's market)

Covent Garden is the de rigueur stop for dedicated tourists.
With its cobbled streets, myriad shops, museums, theatres and
outdoor cafés, it's a great place to spend a day with the masses.
Two markets operate in the central piazza – the Apple Market and the
Jubilee Market. Until 1973, the central Apple Market housed the largest
fruit, veg and flower market in the city. The wholesale operation relo-
cated to Nine Elms, Battersea (see p.136) and in 1980 Covent Garden
Piazza reopened as the capital's biggest craft market.

Apple Market

Designed by Charles Fowler in 1830, the Apple Market is a cheerful apple-red and vanilla-coloured structure housing two levels of (mainly High Street) shops with covered arcades where the market sets up. Apple Market is a must-see stop for many tourists. There are some lovely pieces of artwork and crafts available here with jewellery, wooden toys, clocks, clothing and accessories all well presented and commanding high prices. The emphasis is on quality craftsmanship and since most stallholders actually produce what they are selling, they can accept individual commissions. They even take credit cards as payment at some of the stalls. Jewellery tends to be contemporary and rendered in silver – and much of it with amber or moonstone. The wooden toys, puzzles and puppets make delightful, old-fashioned presents for children and cost about £10 each. On Mondays, the market is devoted to antiques with collectables like teddy bears, prints and jewellery all strongly featured.

Jubilee Market

Definitely the poor relation to the nearby Apple Market, the Jubilee market is unashamedly geared to tourists. However, its setting under a wrought-iron ceiling is delightful. A preponderance of items with names on them signals the kitschy flavour of the place. Still there's a very nice yoghurt and juice bar perfect for getting a blended smoothie and a sandwich stand for a cheap snack. For a bit of fun, stop in at the Chinese astrology stall where you can get a palm reading for £4, a nail health check for £3 or your Chinese zodiac reading for £3. Most of the souvenirs found here are not even British, for instance, a basic boomerang goes for £10. Many visitors, no doubt, are seduced by the heraldry at the Coat of Arms stall where a very helpful man will happily work out your family's crest. Besides these charming diversions, there are plenty of gifts like fancy smelling soaps, ceramic renditions of London street scenes and Union Jack T-shirts. Teenagers may appreciate the cheap, trendy clothing. Mondays see a bit of class injected into the operation when the antique traders set up here.

central

Henrietta Green's Food Lovers' Market

A mecca for food lovers, this market takes place on the second Friday of every month and gathers a good selection of British food producers to the Covent Garden Piazza for a gastronomic funfair. Plenty of tasting can be had for free and there are often cookery demonstrations. Expect a lovely assortment of British cheeses presented by the cheesemakers themselves and heaps of meats, sausages and wild game. The fresh produce, especially the apples and strawberries, is particularly wonderful. They also host a weekend long fair in the autumn and in the spring (usually the last weekend in October and the middle weekend in May). Contact Food Lover's Britain for dates, via e-mail on office@foodlovers-fairs.com or log on to www.foodloversfairs.com.

German Christmas Market

You don't have to travel far to get a glass of mulled wine and an apple strudel. It's all right here at the German Christmas market. Complete with little wooden pine huts serving as stalls, this is the place to find Christmas tree decorations, silly toys, woollen items and sausages. The atmosphere is enchanting and there's even a Santa's grotto for the children. Held for a week before Christmas.

Local Attractions

There are numerous attractions in and around Covent Garden the most prominent being The London Transport Museum (right next to the market). Just ten minutes walk away, on Trafalgar Square, is The National Gallery and next door to that The National Portrait Gallery.

Getting a Stall

Contact the Centre Manager, The Management Office, 41 The Market, Covent Garden, London WC2E 8RF, tel: 020 7836 9136, fax: 020 7240 5770, e-mail: info@coventgardenmarket.co.uk

For the Food Lovers' Market, contact Joanna on 020 7644 0455 or 020 8968 5510; e-mail joanna@foodloversfairs.com

EARLHAM STREET, WC2

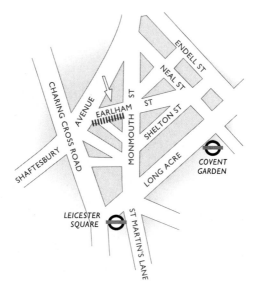

Earlham Street between Shaftesbury Avenue and Seven Dials
Tube: Leicester Square (Northern and Piccadilly); Covent Garden (Piccadilly)
Bus: *14, 19, 24, 29, 38, 176*
Open: *Monday-Saturday 9am-5pm*

Earlham Street Market shares the fate of so many places in Central London, which once served another purpose, but now cater to tourists. Formerly an all-purpose market for the local immigrant community, today the street is filled with flashy, trashy, trendy clothes at one end and beautiful, elegant flowers at the other. Besides the market stalls, there are plenty of excellent little shops such as the Oxfam Original shop selling the high-end stuff that is donated to the charity – expect labels galore at reasonable prices. On the street itself, accessorize with some plastic, fashion sunglasses for a fiver. T-shirts are very popular especially those with witty sayings. A "cheeky monkey" T-shirt will set you back just £5. The majority of garb can be categorised as trendy streetwear so this market is ideal for teenagers and young adults. The cargo pants that are so popular this year are just £10 – a far cry from High Street prices. The flower stalls are to be found near the Seven Dials end of the market.

Refreshment

When you've finished browsing, hop around the corner to the Monmouth Coffee Shop on Monmouth Street for a cup of java in a funky alpine interior. The booths are worth waiting for and the coffee is delectable.

Getting a Stall

Contact Camden Council (see appendix).

LEADENHALL, EC3

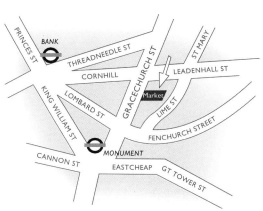

Whittington Avenue (off Gracechurch Street & Leadenhall Street)
Tube: Bank (Central and Northern), Monument (Circle and District)
Bus: 8, 25, 26, 35, 40, 43, 47, 48, 149, 242, 344, 388, 705
Open: Monday-Friday 7am-4pm

Leadenhall has been the site of a market for nearly six hundred years and in that time it was twice destroyed by fire and rebuilt on several occasions. The grand cast-iron and stone structure that stands today was designed by Sir Horace Jones in 1881 and has a wonderful atmosphere with arched thoroughfares leading to a domed central meeting place. The only hitch in this tale of continuity is the fact that Leadenhall market has evolved to the stage where it is not a market at all, but rather a permanent shopping arcade containing many High Street shops including a branch of Jigsaw and Waterstones. It is still an interesting place to visit and there are several very fine greengrocers, fishmongers and butchers within the arcade which continue to sell the kind of produce that has been sold here for centuries.

Another thing that gives this market a unique character is its location in the heart of London's financial square mile with the Lloyds' building designed by Richard Rodgers looming above it. I would encourage a look at this spectacular steel and glass building – from Leadenhall Place you can enjoy the sight of people going up and down in the external glass lifts. If you don't enjoy crowds it's advisable to avoid this area during lunch time when thousands of city folk in suits descend upon the market to get something to eat or do a bit of shopping. Leadenhall is an interesting place to visit on any weekday but is at its best in the weeks running up to Christmas when the food shops are festooned with seasonal fare.

Getting a Stall

All the stalls at Leadenhall are run on a leasehold basis and not available for short term rent.

LEATHER LANE, EC1

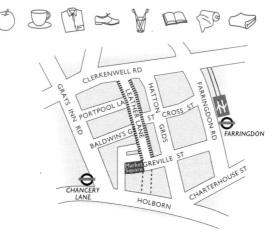

Leather Lane (between Clerkenwell Road and Greville Street)
Tube: Farringdon (Circle and Metropolitan), Chancery Lane (Central)
Bus: 55, 243, 153 (Clerkenwell);
17, 45, 46, 341 (Gray's Inn Road)
Open: Monday-Friday 10.30am-2.00pm

With the closure of Exmouth Market and Farringdon Book Market in recent years, Leather Lane has become the last major market in Clerkenwell. The demise of the other two venues was partly due to the decline in the resident population of Clerkenwell, while Leather Lane has survived by becoming a lunch time market catering for the office workers of the area. Leather Lane is a functional weekday market, but it's still great fun and well worth visiting even if you're not a nine-to-fiver. To avoid the crowds, it's advisable to visit the market between 10.30am and 12 noon before the street fills with people out for a quick shop during their lunch break. The cheap magazine stall on the corner of Clerkenwell Road is a good place to start, with hundreds of slightly out of date mags covering anything from body-building to celebrity gossip for 50p each or 3 for £1. There is also a very good fruit and veg stall here selling the basics as well as more fancy stuff like mange tout and fresh herbs. There are numerous clothes stalls along Leather Lane with one of the best offering great value casual women's cotton slacks for £3 and two stylish cotton tops for £5. Another trader was doing brisk business with a pile of second-hand canvas shorts for only £3 a pair.

Further south, between Portpool Lane and St Cross Street are some of the most interesting stalls with the deli trader stocking some of the fine foods that could once have been bought from the gone but not forgotten Ferraro Continental Food Store. The market changes during the year, on a recent visit in the height of summer the body warmers had disappeared to be replaced by swimwear for £2.99 a go, and there was a stall selling flip-flops for just a few quid. Just opposite the junction with St Cross Street is a charity shop (Camden Age Concern) for those who enjoy bargain hunting. The fabric stall nearby represents excellent value with some large remnants for only a fiver and many cotton fabrics for just £2 per metre.

Further along, Leather Lane has one of the best jewellery stalls in London with simple rings for as little as £5. One customer asked for arm bracelets and from behind the stall emerged a box with a variety of funky designs to choose from. There are several good shoe stalls on Leather Lane, but the busiest was selling women's shoes for only £6 a pair from boxes on the pavement and attracting a small crowd of people looking for a bargain. Another regular trader who deserves special mention is the bedding and towel man who offers two white pillow cases and a kingsize duvet with an attractive embroidered pattern for only £30 and two large cotton bath towels for only £10.

Further south there are numerous stalls selling clothing, shoes, toiletries and funky jewellery. The trader selling bags had some tempting deals with the same small nylon shoulder bag I had paid £10 for on Berwick Street Market the week before on offer here for only £4.99. The shoe stall on this part of the market was also very interesting with good quality ladies dress shoes for a very reasonable £24.99 and casual summer sandals for £10.

The end of the market is marked by a square of stalls between Beauchamp Gardens and Greville Street. This is usually one of the

central

busiest parts of Leather Lane, but on my last visit there were fewer stalls than usual although there were one or two interesting things to be found here. The video stall was still going strong although now most of the stock is in DVD format at £9.99 and the videos have been demoted to a lower table for only £3.99. The young couple selling women's Indian cotton blouses for only a fiver were doing a brisk trade. If you're in need of something a little smarter there was a stall here with women's two-piece office suits from £30. The shoe stall at the back of the square was also good value although only catering for the female of the species.

Refreshment

Being a lunch time market Leather Lane has lots of good places to eat and drink. Hanks Café is a stylish modern place offering good value fare at the Clerkenwell end of the market. For tasty food in a more traditional environment, The Bagel Bakery and The Traditional Plaice fish and chip shop are both old favourites. Shorties, on Cross Street, has come under new management, but still serves excellent value Mediterranean food and a decent capuccino. At the far end of the market on Grenville Street is a traditional kosher/vegetarian sandwich bar which prepares more original dishes than the many anonymous cafés at this end of the market. If you fancy something a little more predictable there is a Pret à Manger in the pedestrian walk way as you head south.

Local Attractions

There are numerous interesting shops in the area. L. Terroni & Sons, just opposite the market on Clerkenwell, is still one of the best Italian deli's in town and one of the last vestiges of Clerkenwell's Italian community. Although the market offers very little in the way of literature, Soho Original Bookshop is a recent addition to the street and carries a good range of discounted books. In terms of tourist attractions, the Sir John Soane's Museum (13 Lincoln's Inn Fields, WC2) nearby is one of the most unusual museums in London.

Getting a Stall

For further details contact Camden Council (see appendix).

LOWER MARSH, SE1

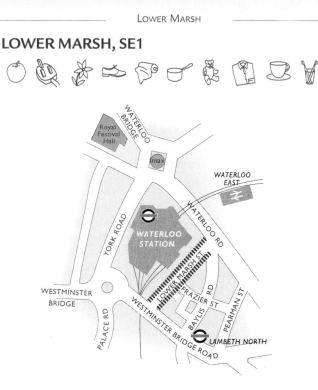

Lower Marsh from Westminster Bridge Road to Baylis Road

Tube: Waterloo (Northern, Bakerloo, Waterloo & City), Lambeth North (Bakerloo)
Rail: Waterloo (take the exit nearest Platform 1, follow the road down and take the underpass into Leake Street)
Bus: 1, 4, 26, 59, 68, 76, 139, 168, 171, 176, 188, 243, 341, 521, X68 (Waterloo Road); 12, 53, 148, 159, 211, 453 (Westminster Bridge Road)
Open: Monday-Friday from around 9am, with market fully operational over lunch time: 11am-2pm; some stall-holders also set up on Saturdays, but the market is a lot more patchy

Having been forcibly down-sized by the demise of the GLC in the eighties (which knocked out a considerable chunk of its lunch time trade), Lower Marsh is no longer the large, vibrant market it was when it used to stretch right into The Cut. The unused stalls piled-up in the courtyard at the Westminster Bridge Road end of the market, are testament to this decline. Despite this, traders on this site have over 150 years of tradition to uphold and a reliable influx of shoppers still passes through the street on a weekday. As with most community markets, utility is the name of the game at Lower Marsh with traders focusing on everyday needs: fruit and veg, household goods and kitchen equipment (check out the deals on pan sets and knives), toiletries, haberdashery and fabric, luggage, children's games and toys, as well as electrical items like personal stereos, radios and cameras. Underwear and socks, bedding plants and flowers, sweets, cards, batteries, women's office wear, shoes, hair accessories, CDs (new releases £11.99), bedding and towels all get a look in too. There are also a few stalls selling African crafts, craft materials and jewellery. The young woman running the wooden crafts stall occasionally raised a titter by shouting out, "genuine Indonesian plastic sold here!" The two Asian men who were selling boxed and apparently as new telephones for £5-£10 were offering a good deal, although one customer thought it prudent to buy a phone with the threat of a violent return in the event of any problems with the product.

Eurostar day-trippers and tourists tend to head north for the civic grandeur of the South Bank complex rather than opt to explore the rumbling, grimy streets at the back of Waterloo, but Lower Marsh is well worth a visit for a glimpse of London at its hybrid best. The street itself is probably more of a pull than the market as waves of commercial development have left a lively blend of trendy boutiques, specialist businesses and traditional, functional shops. Sadly, however, L&C Cohen has recently ceased trading after over 80 years selling men's clothes on Lower Marsh.

central

Refreshment

When it comes to eating, Lower Marsh has lots to offer the visitor. Food stops mirror the hybrid mix of shops, with Marie's Café acting as a greasy spoon during the day and becoming a Thai diner at night. Further afield on Cornwall Road, 'bespoke bakery' Konditor & Cook is crammed with lovingly-crafted cakes, breads and sandwiches and also has a concession in the Young Vic on The Cut if you fancy a sit-down treat. The cavernous Fire Station Bar on Waterloo Road serves solid lunches, or you can opt for a healthy lunch from Coopers Natural Foods (on Lower Marsh) which now has seating rather than the strictly take-away service of former years. If you scoff at the idea of health food and would prefer a liquid lunch, try Cubana at the Waterloo Road end of the market, or the very trendy Ruby Bar in the middle of Lower Marsh.

Local Attractions

Clothing is one of Lower Marsh's fortes, with a number of both first and second-hand shops; try retro boutique Radio Days for impeccably suave clothes, furniture and ephemera, and What The Butler Wore for racks full of stylishly fifties-to-seventies clothes. Those who do not have 20/20 vision should have a look at 20/20 Vision which stocks designer eyewear at well under West End prices. Other interesting units include the well-established classical music shop, Gramex, and the Far East Supermarket, which stocks everything from pak choi to tom yum, as well as great spices and strange packets of things like Great Impression 'losing weight' tea. Those of a literary leaning should not miss Jane Gibberd Secondhand Books (20 Lower Marsh) which is a beautiful little shop and even has a lush garden at the back of the premises, visible through a glass wall. Further afield there is plenty to explore, with Lower Marsh within easy walking distance of the South Bank Centre which includes the Hayward Gallery, the NFT, and the London Eye. The massive IMAX 3-D Cinema is also just around the corner.

Getting a Stall

For further details contact Lambeth Council (see appendix).

PICCADILLY MARKET, W1

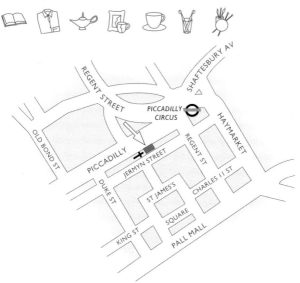

St James's Churchyard, Piccadilly

Tube: Piccadilly Circus (Piccadilly, Bakerloo)
Bus: 8, 9, 14, 19, 22, 38
Open: Tuesday 10am-6pm (antiques),
Wednesday-Saturday 10am-6pm (arts & crafts)

Piccadilly is a huge four lane road which is always crammed with heavy traffic and its pavements are equally busy with pedestrians. The courtyard of St James' Church is for this reason a particularly welcome quiet space amid all the chaos and is the perfect site for this arts and crafts and antiques market. The large wrought iron gates of the church are covered with ivy and act as an effective barrier between the street and the shade of the courtyard. When you enter it's worth looking down to notice the heavy flagstones that cover the floor, quite a few of which still bear inscriptions in memory of those long departed. If you look up there is the spire of the church to admire and whose bells chime into life at the turn of every hour.

On Tuesdays the market is given over to antiques, collectables and bric-à-brac with myriad small items to sift through including pens, paperweights, pictures, stamps, coins, cigarette cards, old medals and antique and second-hand books. Even if you aren't an enthusiastic collector the market on Tuesdays is an interesting spot to visit. The post-card stall is a great place to while away some time with lots of aged postcards to admire – some of which have been completed with accounts of holidays from many years past. The political postcards are particularly fascinating and represent a little piece of history which can often be bought for less than a pound. The coins are also popular although many are just piled into boxes with browsers invited to sift through the old coinage for something of interest. The market is a good place to find fine silverware with several stalls selling cutlery at pretty reasonable prices. One stall offered larger items like clocks, wooden boxes and some very attractive watercolours for between £75 and £85. The stall selling old prints and maps is also a rewarding place to spend some time with all items carefully catalogued and wrapped in cellophane to protect them and offering a particularly well-stocked selection of maps and prints of the capital – most of which originate from the 18th century.

If collectables are not your cup of tea, the market is best visited between Wednesday and Saturday when it is given over to contemporary arts and crafts although a few souvenir stalls also take up residence here. The latter are easily identified as they are resplendent with Union Jack T-shirts, and various models and pictures featuring London buses and red phone boxes. It is easy to sneer at such touristy stuff, but the visitors seem to like it and I still have my plastic Eiffel Tower from a visit to Paris in 1992 – so I will avoid being too sniffy. The stall selling bags and purses is reasonable value with leather bags for about £25 and purses for only £4. Unlike the antiques market, the provenance of goods during the rest of the week is very broad, with a stall selling dolls, watches, badges and medals from Russia, another specialising in goods from Tibet and all things Buddhist and another selling Indian clothing largely made from cotton and in a style that might best be described as ethnic. The watch stall has a more contemporary feel, with modern stainless steel

central

watches from only £10. The scented soap stall is tucked away at the back of the market, but is easy to find by following the smell that exudes from that corner and is a good place to get reasonably priced handmade soaps. One of my favourite stalls is situated at the opposite corner of the market and specialises in colourful modern glassware and jewellery with funky glass rings for only £12. The stall has quite a few devotees and on a recent visit a woman had made a special trip to pick up a few things for friends having visited the stall a few weeks previously.

St James's Market does tend to cater for the many tourists that visit the area, but is still a great place to visit if only to escape from the crowds and enjoy some relative tranquillity in the church courtyard. The church itself is a fantastic example of Wren's work and it is often open if you should wish to have a look around inside.

Refreshment
There is a café attached to the annex of the church which is now run by the Café Nero chain. It's a great place to relax, particularly on fine days when there is seating outside. There are not many alternatives to this café in the area, although if you fancy going very up-market the Ritz is about 5 minutes further west along Piccadilly and does a slap-up tea at a truly exorbitant price.

Local Attractions
Just a little further along Piccadilly is The Royal Academy of Arts which is well worth a visit and is a good place to while away a few hours. The shopping in the area is a little expensive for most of us, but Piccadilly is becoming one of the main streets for bookshops in London and is the site for both the flagship Waterstones store and Hatchards. If you want to visit another market, proceed north up Regent Street and cut through Carnaby Street to Berwick Street Market which is still a great Soho institution (see page 6 for details).

Getting a Stall
If you are interested in having a stall at Piccadilly Market contact the Rector's office on 020 7734 4511 or visit the Rectory (in the court-yard of the church) during market hours.

SMITHFIELD, EC1

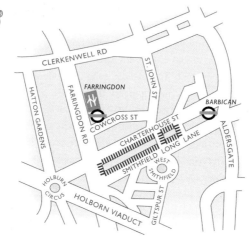

Charterhouse Street

Tube: Farringdon and Barbican
(Circle, Metropolitan and Hammersmith and City)
Bus: 55, 243, (Clerkenwell Road)
Open: Monday-Friday 4am-12noon

Smithfield Market is the last wholesale market in London to remain on its original site and meat has been sold here for over eight hundred years. The present building is an impressive edifice of iron, stone and brick designed by Sir Horace Jones (who also designed Leadenhall Market) and built in 1866. Behind the immutable exterior, however, things have not stayed still and the market has undergone a £70 million redevelopment in recent years.

If you walk through the central archway at the bottom of St John Street and take a look down any of the buyers' avenues the change is easy to see. The interior of the massive Victorian building has been stripped out and, instead of the rather dark chaotic workings of the old market, new avenues have been created with each trader selling meat from modern counters and the meat being unpacked behind glass screens direct from the lorries. These changes were primarily introduced to improve efficiency and conform to hygiene regulations, but they also make this a far more welcoming place for members of the public to shop, if also diminishing some of its spit and sawdust vitality.

Early in the morning all the trade is on a large commercial scale, with wholesalers, butchers and those buying for London's restaurants and hotels doing their business. After about eight in the morning trade begins to slow down and those interested in making smaller purchases can be more easily served. I asked one trader whether he could sell one of his corn-fed chickens, rather than the box of eight that cost £20. His response was friendly and succinct "oh yeah, we always welcome RM", and when he noticed my look of incomprehension he kindly explained "RM means ready money". There are some excellent meaty bargains to be found here making it a worthwhile destination if you have a large carnivorous family and a spacious freezer compartment. Among the bargains was a large box of frozen chicken legs (about thirty legs) for £6.50, while more unusual things like prepared stewing rabbit were only £2.50 per box. Another change in favour of retail customers is the increase in prepared meats and other things like Italian pannetone cakes being sold here. Smithfield is a pleasant and friendly place to shop in the morning and there are usually quite a few people strolling through the well-lit avenues looking for bargains.

Refreshment

There are lots of places to get refreshment in and around the market from early in the morning. Among the more established are The Hope and Sir Loin pub on St John Street (open from 6.30am) and the Fox & Anchor on Chamberhouse Street (open from 7am). There is also a Coffee Republic right on the corner of Cow Cross Street. Also on Cow Cross Street is an excellent veggie café called The Greenway, which is a welcome stop if you've had enough of meat for one morning.

SOUTH BANK BOOK MARKET

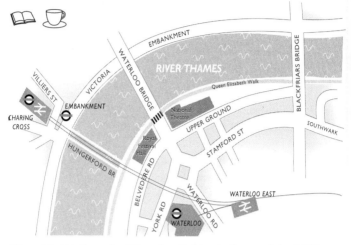

Riverside Walk under Waterloo Bridge in front of the NFT
Tube/Rail: Waterloo (Northern and Piccadilly)
Bus: 1, 4, 26, 68, 59, 76, 139, 168, 171, 172, 176, 188, 243, 341, 521, X68
Open: Daily noon-6pm (winter); 11am-7pm (summer)

It would be hard to imagine a more perfect location for a book market than on the south bank of the Thames, just outside the National Film Theatre (NFT), under the protection of Waterloo Bridge and with a fantastic view of the London skyline. Not only is it a good place to browse for books but, with a broad tree-lined pedestrian "boulevard", it also has a romantic atmosphere. I am not alone in thinking this as, afterall, it was here that Hugh Grant made his declaration of love in the film Four Weddings and a Funeral and I know of at least one couple that carried out a good deal of their courtship here. The secret of the place is that, although it is located in the centre of London, it's spirit and atmosphere is reminiscent of the south bank of the Seine in Paris. After only a few minutes of browsing among the books I feel the urge to don a black polo neck, start smoking Gitanes and buy at least one book concerning existentialism.

The market has around one hundred tables heaving under the weight of thousands of books covering most subjects. Works by all the giants of European literature can be found here including such names as Dickens, Balzac, Henry James, Orwell, Steinbeck and Kafka. If you prefer a good page turner there are enough books by the likes of Jilly Cooper, Jeffery Archer and Catherine Cookson to keep you entertained. This is also a good market to visit for academic and reference books with plenty of philosophy, psychology, art history and architecture. Naturally, being in the heart of the South Bank Centre (the centre offers cutting-edge art exhibitions at the Hayward Gallery, classical and contemporary concerts and dance performances at the Royal Festival and Queen Elizabeth Halls, repertory cinema and the annual London Film Festival at the NFT), there is a good selection of plays, screenplays and books about film and theatre. Biographies are also well represented with anything from Kitty Kelly's prurient treatment of Frank Sinatra to more noble attempts to capture the lives of novelist Grahman Greene or movie star Greta Garbo. There are also a fair few stalls selling mounted prints, usually illustrations taken from old books. The range of illustrations is fairly limited and a good deal of it consists of old maps, but there are sometimes things of interest to be uncovered.

The South Bank Book Market is not the cheapest place to find second-hand books, with most paperbacks selling for around half their new price, but among the thousands of books on offer you can usually find the odd bargain such as the paperback edition of Pevsner's Outline of European Architecture I found recently for a mere £3. Anyway most of the people visiting here are really interested in enjoying the atmosphere and having a browse, rather than trying to save a few quid.

Refreshment
The NFT café is right next to the market, but the food is unexceptional and expensive. You might be better at the coffee bar just outside the National Theatre.

Getting a Stall
There are only ten licenses to sell books on this site, and the current traders have no plans to leave.

STRUTTON GROUND, SW1

Strutton Ground (the south side of Victoria Street)
Tube: St James's Park (Circle, District)
Bus: 11, 24, 148, 211, 507, 705
Open: Monday-Friday 11.30am-3pm

S trutton Ground is a small lunch time market in the heart of Victoria. Every weekday around twenty stalls set up here and await the rush of office workers during the lunch hour. If you don't like crowds it's a good idea to visit this market either before 12 noon or after 2pm. The market offers high quality but basic fruit and veg, cut flowers, cheap DVDs and CDs, and good value office clothing for women with suits starting from £25.

Among the stalls was one doing a brisk business in womens' casual clothing, with all items for £5 and a crowd of office workers sifting through the rails for something in their size. There are several stalls selling fashionable shoes with one offering quality footwear for £5-£15 and the others selling a more limited range of disposable summer sandals for as little as a pound. There's also a stall dealing in branded cosmetics at well below High Street prices that is always popular with the regulars. There are several mixed stalls on the market with one selling underwear and sunglasses, and another stocking bags, belts and batteries at very reasonable prices. The jewellery stall is also great value with a selection of traditional silver jewellery starting from £3.50 and going up to £15. A recent addition to the market is a stall selling nightclothes including Japanese style cotton bathrobes for only £10 and several nightdresses reduced to just a few quid to clear.

Refreshment

Being a lunch time market, there are no end of places to get a drink or a bite to eat. Among the best are The Trio Bar for basic food, Finnegan's Wake public house for a pint, Greens for take-away whole-food, Stiles bakery and the more fancy Le Pain du Jour. At the top end of the market is the long established Laughing Halibut for tradi-tional fish and chips as well as the Express Coffee Co. which does good coffee but is short on seating. The pretentiously named Sandwich Project is a new sandwich bar on the street which serves good coffee.

Local Attractions

There is no book stall on the market, but an Oxfam Bookshop has moved onto the street and offers a fantastic selection of second-hand books at a reasonable price. In terms of tourist attractions the Houses of Parliament are within walking distance east along Victoria Street and Westminster Abbey is just a few minutes west along the same road.

Getting a Stall

For further details contact Westminster Council (see appendix).

TACHBROOK STREET, SW1

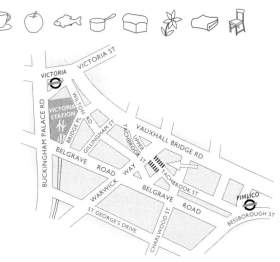

Tachbrook Street between Warwick Way and Churton Street

Tube: *Pimlico (Victoria), Victoria (Victoria, District and Circle)*
Rail: *Victoira*
Bus: *2, 24, 36, 185, 436, C10*
Open: *Tuesday-Friday 9.30am-4.30pm, Saturday 9.30am-4.30pm (some stalls)*

Tachbrook Street Market has seen much better days in its long history dating back to the 19th century. It has now dwindled to just half a dozen stalls selling quality fruit and veg, cut flowers, bedding and towels as well as fresh bread. There have been some encouraging changes in recent years with the arrival of a stall specialising in olives and olive oil and a few dealing in second-hand furniture and knick-knacks, one of which had a good selection of costume jewellery at very reasonable prices. Tachbrook Street is a charming little market and given the appeal of the nearby shops and cafés, well worth making a special effort to visit. This part of Pimlico still has a community atmosphere and sense of place that is a welcome contrast to the soulless office developments and heavy traffic of nearby Victoria.

Refreshment

If you're feeling peckish I strongly recommend a piece of pizza and a cappuccino at Gastronomia Italia, on Upper Tachbrook Street, which also has tables outside on fine days. Bar Fresco, just around the corner on Longmore Street, is also a very good café. If you fancy an alcoholic beverage, The Page is just opposite the market and is a contemporary style pub.

Local Attractions

Despite the subdued nature of the market, the area is still very much worth a visit if only to escape the polluted and crowded mayhem around Victoria Station. If you like hunting for second-hand bargains there are five excellent charity shops in the area: two FARA on Tachbrook Street, Oxfam on Warwick Way, Trinity Hospice Shop on Wilton Road and the wonderful Crusade which has recently moved to Churton Street following the redevelopment of Lower Tachbrook Street.

Getting a Stall

For further details contact Westminster Council (see appendix).

WHITECROSS STREET, EC1

Whitecross Street, between Old Street and Errol Street
Tube: Old Street (Northern); Barbican (Metropolitan and Circle)
Rail: Old Street
Bus: 55, 243, (Old Street)
Open: Monday-Friday 10am-2.30pm

Whitecross Street is a place where several different worlds intermingle, with smart city workers coming here to shop and eat at lunch time and rubbing shoulders with the locals who live in the various housing estates that are dotted around this part of town. The market is not difficult to find: to the north it is directly opposite the derelict but still grand St Bartholomew's Church and to the south loom the huge Barbican Towers. The lunch time market that runs between these landmarks has seen better days and between Monday and Wednesday there are numerous spaces in the parade of stalls, with the market still managing to muster something like its former glory on a Thursday and Friday.

Part of the market is situated under the canopy of the shopping precinct on the corner of Errol Street. The pedestrian square is given over to a handful of large stalls offering bags, CDs, towels and bedding, underwear and a mixture of casual and smart clothing. Among the bargains to be found here were good quality baseball hats for £4, stylish faux leather handbags for only £7.99 and smart two-piece office suits for only £30. The stall selling cheap underwear also had a great selection of modern leather wallets for £4 which were far nicer than they ought to be for such a price.

Further north along Whitecross Street there are a mix of stalls offering all kinds of things including household goods, CDs and DVDs, toys, smaller electrical items and tools and several stalls offering cheap casual and smart clothing. One of the clothing stalls had reduced all garments to £10 and was awash with shoppers in search of a bargain. There is only one fruit and veg stall in the market, but it's a good one offering quality fresh produce although sticking to the basics rather than anything exotic, it also stocks a few garden plants for those that want to look at flora rather than eat it. The stall flogging cheap books and mags is great value with lots of recently published mags for only 50p each, although sadly this stall is vulnerable to the weather and doesn't show up if it's grim. One of the best stalls sells all kinds of things from plastic crates distributed along the pavement including ply-wood models for children for a few quid and mugs for only 50p each.

Whitecross Street is a great lunch time market and as with all such markets it is quiet before noon and closing down by 2.30 in the afternoon. It's an interesting way to while away a lunch time, particularly when followed by a late lunch once the crowds have returned to work.

Refreshment

As well as being home to a string of café's, chippies and take-aways, Whitecross Street boasts a few upmarket eateries: Carnevale, an award-winning vegetarian restaurant serving hot and cold food to eat in or take away; Tassili (on the right, just off the main road on Roscoe Street) serves up Mediterranean-style lunches and snacks; and Pham Sushi is a new sushi restaurant that is always busy at lunch time. The Cosy has been on the street for donkey's years and offers good quality traditional fish and chips. Alternatively, if the weather is fine, buy some take-away, head back up to Old Street, cross the road and sit and eat lunch in the grounds of the ruined St Bartholomew's church.

Local Attractions

There are two major attractions in this part of town one of which is the Barbican Centre which hosts all kinds of arts and entertainments behind its red brick façade. The Museum of London is about ten minutes walk from the market, but is worth the effort being one of the most interesting museums in the capital. It is currently undergoing a vast redevelopment, but is still open to the public.

Getting a Stall

For further details contact Islington Council (see appendix).

NORTH LONDON

Alfie's Antiques Market	48
Bell Street	51
Camden	54
Camden Passage	62
Chalton Street	66
Chapel Market	69
Church Street	71
Hampstead Community Market	75
Hoxton Street	77
Inverness Street	80
Kilburn Square	82
Nag's Head	84
Queen's Crescent	86
Swiss Cottage	88
Wembley Sunday Market	92

north

ALFIE'S ANTIQUES MARKET, NW8

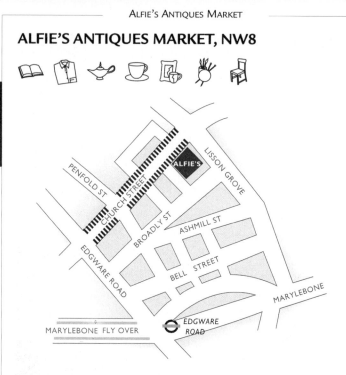

13-25 Church Street
Tube: Edgware Road (Bakerloo)
Bus: *6, 16 18, 27, 98 139, 189*
Open: *Tuesday-Saturday 10am-6pm*

Alfie's is situated in the midst of Church Street Market and acts as a fascinating contrast with its more down-to-earth neighbour. Within this lofty four storey Edwardian building can be found over a hundred dealers selling jewellery, furniture, costume and retro clothing, lighting, tableware, objets d'art, paintings, clocks and books. Among the most interesting things found here on a recent visit were a set of two Italian, cherry wood armchairs re-upholstered in purple velvet and dating from the 1950's. The chairs were wonderful and had a price tag of £1750 which was reasonable given their quality and rarity. Two decent armchairs from Habitat would probably set you back a similar amount and would seem dull in comparison. Similarly the dealer specialising in lighting had a spectacular range of large steel angle-poise lamps for up to £195, which might seem expensive, but these lamps were design classics that looked as though they could last a lifetime.

north

If such things are a little beyond your budget there was solace to be found at a nearby concession where a very tidy little 1950's coffee table was only £35. Likewise, wandering through the labyrinthine maze and particularly on the upper storeys I found plenty of traders dealing in attractive smaller items with lower price tags. There were several good costume jewellery dealers with lots of appealing goodies to sift through for £3-£4.

Another dealer displayed a box with an assortment of bric-à-brac with all items – including a rather sweet little Belgian vase – for only a fiver. There are also a few book dealers at Alfie's with anything from tatty old Penguin paperbacks to elegant leather-bound volumes to be found here. Several art dealers ply their trade here, but I was particularly drawn to the poster dealer with huge French advertising posters of the 1920's and 30's adorning his walls. A large poster was several hundred pounds, but Gallic style is an expensive commodity.

One of the best things about Alfie's is the charm of the place. The dealers are friendly, knowledgeable and occasionally eccentric, the building is huge with numerous staircases and various levels within each storey and there is even an iron staircase with glass roof and a small water feature on the ground floor. Another good thing about Alfie's is its diversity with lots of 20th century items as well as the more traditional antiques for which it is better known.

Refreshment

Alfie's has an excellent roof top café which does a selection of Mediterranean food as well as established British favourites and has seating both inside and out.

Local Attractions

The main attraction in this part of town is Church Street Market (see page 71) and the much diminished Bell Street Market (see page 51).

Getting a Stall

For further details contact Alfie's office on 020 7723 6066.

BELL STREET, NW1

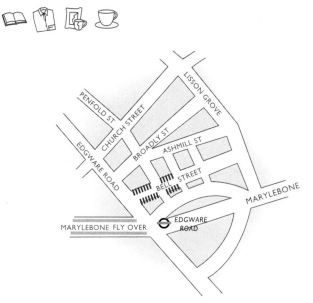

Western end of Bell Street (between Edgware Rd and Penfold St)
Tube: Edgware Road (District, Metropolitan and Bakerloo)
Bus: 6, 7, 15, 16, 18, 23, 36, 98
Open: Saturday 8am-4pm

Bell Street is now a very small flea market with only around three stalls showing up here on a Saturday. The market was not always this small and the few traders that continue here are keen to talk about the market's past – when it was necessary to turn up early to get a stall, and Bell Street attracted crowds of tourists in search of unusual momentoes of their visit to London. It's a shame that the market has hit such hard times, because flea markets of this kind are few and far between in the capital with Brick Lane Market on a Sunday and the north end of Portobello Road on a Saturday being the most notable examples.

51

Bell Street may be a shadow of its former self but it is still an interesting market with the stalls that do turn up offering a great selection of second-hand clothes, books and bric-à-brac. The second-hand clothes stall had some great buys including a Gap blouse for £3, jeans for £3-£4 and several rails with clothing reduced to £1. Jock is a regular here and offers a mixed assortment of things which included a set of golf clubs for only £10, a good quality power drill for £20 and a collection of old framed pictures for just a few pounds each. It would have been easy to conclude that these two stalls were the entire market, but further along Bell Street was a third trader offering a bizarre assortment of old books and bric-à-brac in splendid isolation. The stall had all kinds of strange things like a pair of wooden glasses, an old fish tank and a massive enamel bread bin, with most items being sold for 50p.

Bell Street is a market that needs support. All the people I spoke to were angry at Westminster Council for enforcing laws in an overly strict and officious manner. The main complaint is that the allotted space of 6ft x 4ft is far is too small for a flea market stall. Second-hand traders offer a diverse range of goods and generally add very little mark-up on each item, and so it is almost impossible for such a trader to cover the £30 rent from such a small pitch. Enforcing traders to stay within these narrow markings on the road may be justified when space is being fought over, but makes no sense when most of the street is empty. Another accusation is that Westminster Council has driven the small group of regular fly-pitchers off the market by confiscating their goods. Fly-pitchers are those small traders who sell a limited range of clobber from a blanket on the street without paying rent. Although they are strictly illegal they are a harmless bunch, add to the diversity of a flea market and are generally tolerated at markets like Camden Passage and Portobello Road. The use of a van full of market inspectors to remove these vulnerable people from the pavement seems a waste of public money and will seriously damage the future of the market. The council is not the only reason for the decline of this market, but it is probably the main one.

Local Attractions

The main attraction of this part of town is Bell Street's sister market – Church Street (see page 71 for further details) which is accessible via Penfold Street. Penfold Street also has a lovely public garden which is a great place to relax on fine days. Bell Street has lost many of its most interesting shops in recent years, but the Vintage Wireless Co. is a real treat for hi-fi buffs and is still going strong.

Refreshment

The Green Man pub is a long established drinking hole on the corner of Bell Street which serves a reasonable pint. If you prefer non-alcoholic refreshment try La Belle's snack bar which is a little further along Bell Street and does a mean cappuccino.

Getting a Stall

For further details contact Westminster City Council (see appendix).

CAMDEN, NW1

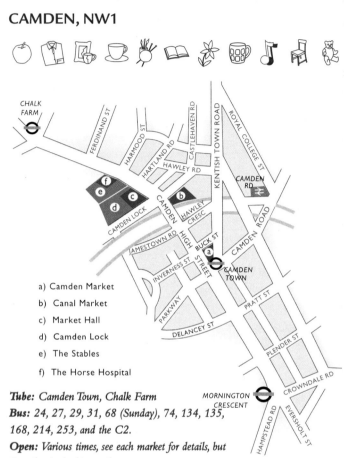

a) Camden Market
b) Canal Market
c) Market Hall
d) Camden Lock
e) The Stables
f) The Horse Hospital

Tube: Camden Town, Chalk Farm
Bus: 24, 27, 29, 31, 68 (Sunday), 74, 134, 135, 168, 214, 253, and the C2.
Open: Various times, see each market for details, but Saturday is the biggest day

Six markets make up the Camden empire of outdoor and indoor trade. It is certainly one of London's busiest markets and has a big following on weekends. On Sundays, Camden Town tube station is 'exit only' so as so cope with the masses flooding the streets. Crowds are de rigueur here with the weekends seeing the worst of the crush. Everything from furniture to jewellery is for sale here – antique and contemporary. You will also find health food, retro clothing, clubwear, and stupid souvenirs. Camden Lock and The Stables offer more in the way of artisan's wares whereas Camden Market and Camden Canal Market have way more tat. Camden Lock Market is the best place to find jewellery handmade in the UK. The rest of the markets tend to carry silver jewellery from Asia and amber from the Baltics. If you are looking to kit yourself out in a corset, tall lace-up boots, wigs or other fetish wear, you'll find plenty of it here especially at the Stables Market. Or relive the 70s' punk movement by buying a pair of tight plaid trousers and Doc Martens. Vintage clothing from earlier eras is plentiful as well.

Along the way, plenty of head shops, tattoo studios, pubs, and chain restaurants offer diversion along Camden High Street and Chalk Farm Road. In general, the shops are open 10am to 6pm daily. For original artwork straight from the artist, try Camden Lock Market Hall and the Stables Market.

Quirky characters and punky teens flock here for the funky vibe that Camden embodies so well. Alternative – whether it be earth-loving hippies or pale-faced goths – is the mainstream in Camden. In fact, the bulk of bodies are young urbanites from all corners of the globe. If you are young and trendy, Camden is your mecca. Despite this, the place does also fill up with curious tourists, fashionistas sourcing unique clothing and accessories and neighbourhood residents out for a shopping trip. Thursdays and Fridays are quieter than the raucous, packed out weekends.

Refreshment

Besides the plethora of food stalls in the market, which as expected, serve a variety of international dishes, there are plenty of restaurants. All the big chains have a piece of the pie here from Belgo to Pizza Express to Wagamama. Dingwalls/Bar Risa in Middle Yard at Camden Lock Market is a great place for a fair-weather pint. The roof terrace has superb views of the canal. Camden Lock has the best collection of outdoor eating and drinking spots. For a post-shopping escape, head to Marine Ices at 8 Haverstock Hill near Chalk Farm tube. Not just a purveyor of fine ice creams, but also of cheap and tasty Italian pastas, pizzas and salads.

Local Attractions

The canal path that runs through Camden can be picked up at Camden Lock. It's a great way to escape the crowds and runs down to Little Venice in the west and Islington in the north. For a pleasant, relaxed trip down the waterway, hop on a canal boat at the Camden Lock stop. The boat route extends between London Zoo in Regent's Park and Little Venice. Try Regent's Canal Waterbus (tel. 020 7482 2550), Jason's Trips (tel. 020 7286 6752), or Jenny Wren's Canal Boat Cruises (tel. 020 7485 4433).

Camden Market

Camden High Street, south of Buck Street

Open: Thursday-Sunday 9am-5:30pm

This is the first market that you hit as you exit from Camden tube station. A cluster of stalls vies for attention here. Between the naff tie-dyed shirts and Rastafarian hats for teenagers hoping to add interest to their wardrobe, there are plenty of reasonably priced garments that could be worn outside of Camden Town. Casual streetwear is especially good here with many things for less than a tenner. A handful of stalls sell originally designed clothing and silver jewellery, but most of the merchandise is the made-in-China variety: cheap and cheerful. Besides the music blasting from practically every stall (there will be something to suit your taste), the record sellers offer vinyl and CDs for competitive prices.

If you don't like crowds, you should visit on Thursday or Friday when it's slightly quieter. The Weekend crowds will send any claustrophobic into a tailspin. The added bonus of visiting towards the end of the week is that, since there is less traffic, the merchants are more amenable to bargaining.

Getting a Stall

Camden Market 020 7351 5353

You can turn up at the market office (at the back of the market) any day and get a stall. Weekend stalls are much harder to get and you need to apply for a weekday stall first then work your way up to qualify for a weekend pitch.

Inverness Street Market
See entry on page 80

Camden Canal Market
Northeast of the canal, and south of Castle Haven Road
Open: Friday-Sunday 9.30am-6.30pm
This market started out as a general market, but today trades in a mixed bag of products. Pass through the covered entrance to find about 150 stalls and shops selling trendy fashions (of course) and the accessories to go with them. One specialist here sells and exchanges computer games, and another repairs and upgrades computers. Beyond the contemporary stuff, there are a host of merchants dealing in retro clothing. It's worth popping in here to seek out some unique items to enliven your wardrobe. Food stalls run the culinary gamut from Thai to baked potatoes.

Getting a Stall
Camden Canal Market Office
Stables Market Ltd,
27 Stanley Sidings, Chalk Farm Road, NW1 8AH
Tel: 020 7485 5511

Camden Lock Market
Northwest of Camden Lock

Open: Saturday-Sunday 10am-6pm with some shops and stalls open Tuesday-Sunday 10am-6pm

This market was the epicentre of the rise of the Camden markets empire. Started in 1975, this market retains many of its original structural features, but has been updated with the times and is a great place to shop for original items. The traders here are savvy and present their goods well. This is not a mishmash of junk, rather an elegant collection of rather good quality and interesting merchandise. To get here walk up Camden High Street past the other markets and take a left. As its name suggests, it sits right next to the canal.

The market itself is a warren of courtyards and buildings. Divided into five parts, there is the Market Hall with three levels of shops and three open-air squares called East Yard, Middle Yard and West Yard. Between the Stables Market and the Market Hall lies the last bit of the market – Camden Lock Place.

The Market Hall, a Victorian-style covered market, houses about 70 stalls that are open daily, and has an entrance off Chalk Farm Road. Original paintings and photography are for sale here and a variety of craftspeople sell their wares here too. Look out for the handmade stationery, notebooks, and photo albums fashioned from recycled paper, or the artistic slate clocks. The Market Hall's second floor houses shops and is the place to track down designer fashions and collectables as well as the more mysterious palmists and tarot card readers. If you want permanent jewellery, stop by the body-piercing specialist. The third floor is used as office space. As with the rest of the greater market, there are no shortage of imported goods for sale from Peruvian textiles to South American wooden carvings. These specialists cater to the shopper looking for ethnic chic, without going to the trouble of travelling. Boost your spirituality with a Tibetan Buddha or a Hindu deity direct from Nepal. Designer clothing is a big deal here and, occasionally, the local designers organise fashion shows. Fairygothmother, occupying a proper shop at 8 East Yard, is an exceptionally interesting outlet dedicated to fetish wear.

There is also a very good stall here with an assortment of wooden games and balls for children – a good distraction thus avoiding awkward questions regarding fetish clothing.

East Yard, which is open daily, has about 50 stalls and sits next to the canal and Camden High Street. The outdoor square that is the West Yard is home to several international food stalls and about 80 stalls selling mostly crafts and ethnic chic items like rugs, paper lanterns, and wooden toys. Canal boats leave for their trips to London Zoo or Little Venice from here. Many of the pubs and restaurants here have open-air seating so as better to watch the comings and goings along the canal. Middle Yard has weekday shops and about two dozen stalls at the weekend.

The cobbled alley of Camden Lock Place also has weekday shops and about 40 stalls at the weekend. For inexpensive made-to-measure wedding dresses, stop by Henry & Daughter, which also stocks vintage clothing. There are plenty of homewares merchants here too selling everything from clocks to ridiculous statues to bedding.

Getting a Stall

Camden Lock Market Office
56 Camden Lock Place, West Yard, NW1 8AF
Tel: 020 7284 2084
You can turn up at the market any day and get a stall. On weekdays, meet the market manager at the East Yard at 9.45am to see what's available. On weekends, meet at Middle Yard at 9.30am. Prices start at £10 for a Monday skyrocketing to £45 for a Saturday or Sunday.

north

The Stables Market
West of Chalk Farm Road and opposite Hartland Road
Open: Saturday-Sunday 9am-5pm

The Stables Market, housed in former stables used by the horses that pulled the barges up the canal, is the other Camden superstar sharing the spotlight with Camden Lock market. A whopping 350 stalls and shops are open here at the weekend. Here you'll find retro clothes, jazz records and furniture as well as ethnic wares like batik fabrics and kilims. Good old-fashioned second-hand items get a look in here too. The Stables Market lies past the train bridge at the end of Camden High Street. Clothing aplenty can be found here from über-hip urban wear to 1950s day dresses and old wool suits for dapper gentlemen. Biba Lives Vintage Clothing will even use old patterns to fashion new clothing just for you. The vintage retailers are housed in the Arches around the Piazza in the Gin House, which was once a Gilbey's Gin shop. As recycled goods are popular in the markets here, it's no surprise that there is one maker (Jarabosky) dedicated completely to making furniture from old railway sleepers.

Antiques and collectables are sold in the Horse Hospital and Antiques Passage sections of the market. For snacks, take your pick from the world's cuisines at the various food stalls.

As we went to press, the market was in the midst of a plan to upgrade. While much of it will remain the same, there are plans to increase it by another 300 shops and stalls and fill it with more leisure facilities using a disused portion in the southwestern part of the Stables adjacent to Camden Lock Place. An upgrade to the basement space below the Piazza is also planned. That area will house bookshops, an Internet café, and a garden. The idea is also to prolong the hours of the market by bringing in late-night venues like bars, clubs, and restaurants.

Getting a stall
Stables Market Office
Stables Market Ltd, 27 Stanley Sidings, Chalk Farm Road, NW1 8AH
Tel: 020 7485 5511

CAMDEN PASSAGE

Opposite Islington Green at the junction of Upper Street and Essex Road, Islington, N1

Tube: Angel (Northern)
Bus: 38, 56, 73, 341 (Essex Road); 4, 19, 30, 43, (Upper Street)
Open: Wednesday and Saturday 7am-3pm (antique market); Thursday 8:30am-6pm (book market); Sunday 10am-2pm (farmer's market)

L ooking like a centuries' old street untouched by the modern world save for the cross streets intersecting it, Camden Passage takes a step back in time both with its adorably squat shop fronts and its antique merchandise. However, the market has only been in operation since the '60s when Islington was in its nascent period of gentrification. Today the same antique shops serve the rather wealthy denizens of this desirable neighbourhood and antique hunters travel to visit the shops as well as the market so there's always a lively atmosphere even on non-market days.

On Wednesday and Saturday, antiques and ornaments both junky and attractive line the market. Some sellers have tables, and others display their items on blankets or cloths right on the pavement. In bad weather, most of the market huddles under a purpose-built shelter on the northern end of the market.

Silver items are ubiquitous from frames to cutlery to tableware. This is no bargain hunter's paradise either – prices are negotiable but tend to be high. In most cases, you can be guaranteed of quality and authenticity. Some sellers are clearly selling bric-à-brac rather than antiques, but these are self-evident by their low prices, inferior quality and modern design. In general, however, if you are wanting to kit out your house or looking for gifts there are plenty of beautiful pieces of sparkly jewellery, art deco-style lamps, china tea sets and objets d'art.

At the southern end of the market stands the Pierrepont Arcade – another covered portion of the market with al fresco stalls and an indoor maze of units selling little bits and pieces like stamps and military medals.

On the way from the northern stalls to the southern stalls, you'll find a lovely collection of little shops selling prints, furniture and antique dresses. Annie's Vintage Clothes and Cloud Cuckoo Land at the junction with Charlton Place both sell dreamy dresses and accessories from a time gone by. Annie's has a bent towards Victorian era and early 19th-century clothing while Cloud Cuckoo Land sells wonderfully exuberant 1940s, '50s and '60s garb. The street also houses a few shops selling sumptuous art nouveau and art deco jewellery as well stallholders who hawk similar decorative items.

The book market on Thursdays has a completely different feel. While the antique market sells mostly upmarket items to tourists and well-to-do antique hunters, the book market is far more egalitarian. Hardbacks sell for £4 and paperbacks go for a £1 or less. Don't expect decorative antiquarian tomes, but rather popular titles from well-known writers as well as books on travel, art, cooking and history.

On Sundays, foodies gather for the top-notch Islington Farmer's Market – London's first farmer's market which opened in 1999. Spring, summer and early autumn see the best markets when there is a profusion of fresh vegetables and fruits like chard and apples in the autumn; strawberries in the summer and unbelievably tasty Isle of Wight tomatoes from spring until late autumn. The winter market resurrects its share of subterranean vegetables like potatoes and other hearty foods like kale. The bakery stalls near the Camden Head pub sell a delightful, fattening assortment of chocolate cakes and buttery patisserie. The range of breads beats any supermarket or High Street bakery – find rye, sourdough, rosemary, potato and more. The apple stall sells fresh pressed apple juices in a variety of mixes – apple and strawberry is particularly good. The meats range from game to homemade sausages and freshly caught crab and other local seafood. Eggs and goat cheeses are also available and inexpensive annuals and colourful bouquets of flowers are the name of the game at the flower stall. The food market is a delight to the senses and the market stalls are usually manned by the growers themselves who are more than happy to share their expertise with customers.

Refreshment

A stop at the Camden Head pub with its original Victorian swirly etched glass windows and burgundy velvet banquette seating is the perfect end to a market trip. There's a small terrace with picnic benches for warm weather drinking. The only unfortunate facet to this otherwise stunning pub is the flashing game machines in the corner. For more sustenance, simply step out to Upper Street running parallel to Camden Passage to find a plethora of restaurant and cafés serving everything from Thai to French food.

Getting a Stall

For a stand at the antiques market phone 020 7359 0190.
Further details about the Farmers' Markets can be found by phoning 020 7704 9659, also refer to the farmers' markets section on page 232.

CHALTON STREET, NW1

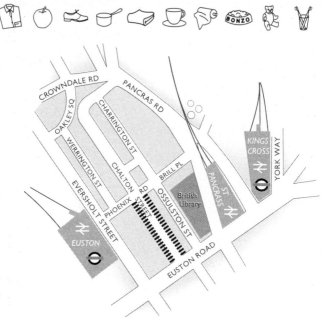

Chalton Street, between Euston Road and Churchway

Tube: *Euston (Northern, Victoria), King's Cross (Piccadilly, Metropolitan, Circle, Northern)*

Bus: *10, 18, 30, 73 (Euston Road)*

Open: *Friday 12noon-2pm*

Chalton Street and its Friday market are easily missed being just off the busy Euston Road. Despite the prestige of the nearby British Library, this area – known as Somers Town – is a poor and rather run-down part of London. The majority of shops are boarded up or empty, making the Friday market a much anticipated event for the local Indian and Pakistani communities who live on the surrounding estates and who, along with the local office workers, comprise the majority of this market's custom.

The market used to run throughout the week, but cutting it down to a Friday lunch time has condensed a week's slow activity into a hectic shopping experience packed into the lunch time hours. Among the twenty or so stalls, there's a lot to catch the eye including basic fashion clothing, shoes, fabrics by the metre, pet food and toys, exotic fruit and veg with plenty of fresh herbs, good value kitchenware and a stall specialising in household cleaning materials and toiletries at a fraction of High Street prices. The large beach towels sold at the towel and bedding stall for just £5 were a good deal as were the women's bags sold in large piles from a couple of tables for just £2 each. There are several good fabric stalls with one at the far end of the market (away from Euston Road) always busy with local Asian women sifting through the reams – many of which are priced at £1 per metre. The shoe stall at the far end of the market is a regular attraction and offers a good selection of ladies footwear for a fiver a pair.

Chalton Street is strong on basic street clothing, but most of the stuff on offer is of the cheap and cheerful variety aimed at the limited pockets of the neighbourhood. For example, most T-shirts are about £2 each and it's very difficult to find one for over a fiver. Value and low price being the name of the game, the old man at the end of the market was doing a roaring trade in an assortment of disparate things from jumbo packs of toilet roll for just £1 to attractive, large enamel flower pots for the same price.

Chalton Street is still an interesting market to visit on a Friday lunch time. Although most of the retail shops have closed, there are lots of cafés catering for the office workers of the area on their lunch breaks making the market a good place to shop and then relax afterwards with a good cappuccino or something to eat.

Refreshment

Café Bella is a fancy establishment at the Euston Road end of the market, but next-door is the more basic and good value King's Café. Just opposite these two is the Empire Café which is a long established traditional caff. Terra Brasil is a very friendly Brazilian café which does a very decent lunch for only £5.50, but tends to charge a lot for its juices. Pinner Café is another good value caff just a few doors down.

Local Attractions

The only major attraction in this part of town is the wonderful British Library which is just a few minutes walk east along Euston Road.

Getting a Stall

For further details contact Camden Council (see appendix).

CHAPEL MARKET, N1

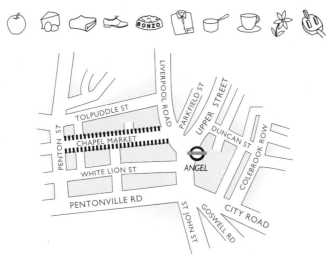

Between Liverpool Road and Penton Street
Tube: Angel (Northern)
Bus: *4, 19, 30, 38, 43, 56, 73, 341, 419 (Islington High Street);*
153, 274 (Tolpuddle Street); 214, 394 (Pentonville Road)
Open: *Tuesday to Saturday 9am-6pm; Thursday and Sunday 9am-4pm*

At the start of the road, this solid local market competes with neighbouring giants – Sainsbury's, Woolworth's and Marks and Spencer (not to mention the Angel shopping centre across the street). Fruit and veg, boldly hawked by poetic stallholders, punctuate the entire market from start to finish. Stick to local goods and what's in season and you'll find good deals on tasty produce. Other stalwarts of the market include stalls full of household products like cleaning potions and electrical goods. Black bin bags come in rolls of 20 for just £1 and you can find cheap DIY tools and other necessities. Trendy fashion such as sweatsuits and the latest shoe styles can all be sourced here as well. The look is definitely geared towards the teen and stylish young market. Inexpensive luggage, handbags and heaps of leather accessories are offered by a handful of market stallholders while speciality stalls stock everything from lace and trimmings to pet supplies, French cheeses, olives, curtains and bedding. The plant stall in the middle of the market is run by a knowledgeable gardener and stocks copious amounts of inexpensive greenery. The make-up of the market varies day to day, but shoppers will find the basic food, flowers, clothes and household goods on all days. Weekends are when the market is at its busiest and best.

After the market, the retail possibilities continue in the shop lining Chapel Street selling sporting goods, beauty products, clothes and shoes for adults and children.

Refreshment

The sweet smell of crêpes and deep-fried doughnuts wafts through the air – these make pleasant treats for hungry shoppers. The baked potato stall offers a heartier alternative and if you want to sit down, Euphorium Bakery can't be beaten for excellent pastries, sandwiches and coffee. Their bread is worth taking home. Other eateries offer everything from eels to curries to pastas. Off the beaten path but nearby on Penton Street is the outstanding Olga Stores, a cramped Italian deli selling scrumptious Italian meats, cheeses and dry goods. The Agricultural is fine for a pint.

Local Attractions

The Crafts Council offices and gallery are just around the corner from the market on Pentonville Road and holds regular exhibitions. Another interesting exhibition space which has the added attraction of a very good café, is the Candid Arts Trust at 3 Torrens Street – just behind Angel tube. The gallery hosts regular exhibitions – phone 020 7837 4237 for their current programme.

Getting a Stall

For further details contact Islington Council (see appendix).

CHURCH STREET, NW8 & W2

Church Street from Edgware Road to Lisson Grove

Tube: Edgware Road (District, Metropolitan and Bakerloo)
Bus: 6, 16, 18, 98 (Edgware Road); 139, 189 (Lisson Grove)
Open: Tuesday-Saturday 9am-5pm

Church Street Market occupies a relatively central location, but few people outside the immediate area actually visit it and if they do it is usually by accident in the process of visiting the more famous Alfie's Antique Market which lies at the Lisson Grove end of the street. For this reason, Church Street Market has managed to maintain a friendly community feel, with lots of the stall-holders taking time out to have a natter with regular customers on quiet weekdays. On Saturdays the market massively increases in size with stalls extending the entire length of Church Street and the crowds making it a very exciting experience, but offering traders little time for a leisurely chat.

north

This part of the Edgware Road (just past the Marylebone fly-over) is pretty down at heel and many of the stalls concentrate on the cheap and cheerful rather than better quality goods. There are for this reason lots of good deals to be found with the £5 shoe stall at the Edgware Road entrance to the market always popular with locals looking for footwear. Church Street is a good market to stock up on basic fresh fruit and veg, but there is not much of the exotic on offer. Likewise, there are now two fresh fish stalls on the street, but they are still concentrating on everyday fare like cod, haddock and salmon with only one or two of the more exotic fish showing their scaly faces here. Further along at the junction with Penfold Street are two of the market's established stalls. The young man selling farm fresh eggs, jars of honey and fruit cake has been here for quite a few years and before that his mother ran the same traditional wooden stall. Offering a more high-tech range of items is the nearby stall with new and boxed electrical goods like televisions, breadmakers and food processors. It was here that one lucky punter picked up a small Kitchen Devil vacuum cleaner for only £20.

Although many of the clothes on offer on Church Street are cheap and tacky, there are several stalls selling interesting stuff such as the one displaying a wide range of designer T-shirts (probably copies) for only a tenner and the stall offering quality leather belts for between £6 and £10. Other items for sale include pet food and toys, household goods, children's clothes, fresh flowers, underwear, bedding and towels and several good value bag stalls stocking anything from rucksacks to suitcases.

At the junction with Salisbury Street, Church Street undergoes a subtle transformation as modern buildings give way to well preserved 19th century shop fronts, many of them dealing in fine antiques. It is at this part of the market that you'll find Alfie's Antiques Market with four floors of antiques and a roof-top café. Outside the building a few fly-traders used to sell knick-knacks and jewellery, but this added attraction to the market has been put to an end by Westminster Council. It's a pity because this part of the market would benefit from a few junk stalls to compliment the many antique shops, but the market itself changes very little despite the change in surroundings. The best thing about this part of the market is the excellent fabric stall selling basic material for as little as 50p a metre. It is also here that one of the strangest stalls can be found selling new fishing equipment, binoculars, amplifiers for public speaking with microphones and a variety of medical things like stethoscopes and devices for measuring blood pressure. I have never encountered such a stall before at a market and the Russian stall-holder was attracting quite a lot of interest although most visitors to his stall shared my bemusement.

Refreshment

Church Street has no smart restaurants but is awash with simple, good value eating places. Among the most popular on Church Street are the falafel stall (reflecting the large Middle-Eastern community in the area), and the prawn stall just after the junction with Penfold Street which is easy to find because of the delicious aroma of prawns and garlic cooking. The Market Grill which serves both English and Thai food is a popular place on market days with a surprising number of burly market traders prefering a bowl of Thai noodles to a traditional fry-up. For a coffee in a more stylish environment try Cali Café, near Alfie's Antiques Market. Alfie's also has a very pleasant roof-top café which does great food and has seating both inside and out. If you want a pint look out for The Traders Inn which is a popular traditional boozer.

Local Attractions

On Saturdays Bell Street Market is five minutes' walk south along Penfold Street and, although a little past its best, should still not be missed by bargain hunters (see page 51). Alfie's Antiques Market is also well worth a visit with its fabulous collection of clothes, pictures, jewellery, furniture and books (see page 48 for further details).

Getting a Stall

For further details contact Westminster City Council (see appendix).

HAMPSTEAD COMMUNITY MARKET, NW3

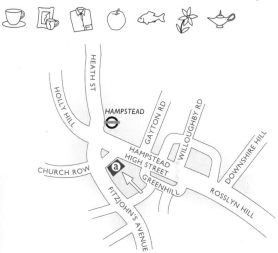

Hampstead Community Centre, 78 Hampstead High Street
Tube: Hampstead (Northern)
Bus: 46, 268
Open: Saturday-Sunday 10am-6pm, and Bank Holidays

The only compelling reason to pay a visit to this market is to get a drink without having to cram into one of Hampstead's homogenised, over-priced coffee bars. Beverages and home-made cakes are consumed sitting on school chairs arranged around a little cluster of tables which makes a nice hideout in which to escape the gorgeous hoards of the High Street. About eight stalls set up in this miniature village hall on a Saturday, offering an oasis of genteel calm and an effective antidote to NW3's air of well-groomed uniformity.

The Community Market used to sell crafts, but is now largely given over to small antiques, collectables and bric-à-brac, supplemented by a wholefood stall and a few tables of expensive new clothing. Although small, interesting things can be found here such as a well made kimono for £35, and a simple 3-piece silver tea service for £30. The elderly ladies that sell collectables and bric-à-brac make an effort presenting their wares and one was particularly proud of her display of fans. The sedate atmosphere of the place is not to everyone's taste, but it has retained a community spirit Hampstead High Street often seems to have lost: friends chat next to racks stuffed with local information leaflets or pass the time of day with the tea ladies. Like the goods inside the market, the fruit, fish and nuts stalls which flank it in an adjacent passage aren't going to pull in punters from outside the immediate area. Produce is top-notch: scrubbed, beautiful and no doubt delicious – but all at NW3 prices.

Local Attractions

'Exclusivo' is a second-hand designer clothes shop just opposite the market. Ignore the dreadful Euro-tat name and head on in for a good rummage. There is also a good Oxfam shop on Gayton Road which is worth a visit for designer cast-offs. For more antiques and collectables the Hampstead Antique and Craft Emporium is just around on Heath Street.

Getting a Stall

For further details contact the Community Centre on 020 7794 8313 or e-mail hcc.camden@virgin.net.

HOXTON STREET, N1

Hoxton Street, between Falkirk Street and Nuttall Street

Tube: Old Street (Northern)

Rail: Old Street

Bus: 55 (Old Street); 67, 149, 242, 243 (Kingsland Road)

Open: Monday-Saturday 9am-4pm (main day Saturday)

Hoxton has a reputation for being ultra-trendy, but the fashion, and money that goes with it, does not extend further north than Hoxton Square. The contrast is most apparent on a busy Saturday when you can walk along Hoxton Street through the busy market full of locals from the surrounding estates doing their shopping and then carry on into Hoxton Square where trendies, models and photographers can be found discussing their latest "project" over a cappuccino. Although the two worlds are just a few minutes walk from each other there is little sign that they mix. It's a pity that the fashionable people that hang out on Hoxton Square and no doubt espouse

77

working-class solidarity, are not to be seen shopping at one of London's traditional street markets.

During the week it would be hard to tell that a market trades on Hoxton Street for just a handful of fruit and veg pitches and the occasional clothing stall show up. It is really on a Saturday that the market takes over, with the street turned into a pedestrian area between the corner of Shenfield Street and Nuttall Street. On a Saturday the market has a real atmosphere with crowds milling between the various stalls featuring a decent selection of street fashion, fruit and veg, flowers, bedding and towels, underwear, shoes, bags, CDs and DVDs and a solitary fresh fish stall.

The market does not have a spectacular range of clothing, but among the unexceptional stalls some good deals and some reasonable quality goods could be found. One stall offered clothing sold in large piles with branded sports clothes for £7 a garment, cotton pajamas for just £5 a go and an assortment of casual clothes for £3. Another popular clothing stall stocked end of season ranges and slight seconds from Topshop for £5-£7. One men's stall stood out with a selection of quality clothing with labels such as Burberry and Lacoste at well below High Street prices. The market is also good for cheap fashion items that are a low-commitment purchase for a night out with skimpy summer shirts for just £3 and mid-length skirts for £5. Other throw-away purchases included attractive summer sandals which probably would not last long but were still good value for only a fiver.

The rest of the market tends to reflect the everyday needs of the local population with the emphasis on low prices rather than quality or diversity. The fruit and veg is fresh but basic, the CDs and DVDs are reasonably priced but only very mainstream stuff, and the duvet covers and towels are mostly in garish colours and synthetic fibres. Likewise the cosmetics are all very cheap and sold quite brazenly as copies with perfumes going for only £4 a bottle. The toy stalls are also stocked with inexpensive plastic stuff, most of which will not survive very long in the hands of the average sprog. The household goods stalls are all dirt cheap and you can't go wrong with large rolls of dustbin bags for just £1 and two face clothes for the same price.

There have been two changes to the market in recent years, one of which being the rise of the huge "gherkin" which now dominates the skyline to the South and helps remind visitors that this working class area is not far from the wealth of the City. The other change is the regrettable disappearance of the second-hand stalls that were once a welcome presence at the northern end of the market.

Refreshment

For something to eat, try either F. Cooke for pie and mash, Café des Amis for a baguette sandwich or one of the market's many greasy spoons for a solid lunch for around £4. There is also a very popular West Indian stall on the junction with Shenfield Street which does delicious barbecue food.

Local Attractions

There are several good shops on Hoxton Street including the Olde Hoxton Curios junk shop and an excellent bookshop at the southern end of the street called the Hoxton Book Depository. Hoxton Market no longer trades in second-hand goods, but if you are looking for interesting junk visit Kingsland Waste (see page 200) which is ten minutes walk along Kingsland Road. Hoxton Square has lots of bars and several fashionable art galleries including White Cube 2 at number 48.

Getting a Stall

For further details contact Hackney Council (see appendix).

INVERNESS STREET, NW1

Between Camden High Street and Arlington Road
Tube: Camden Town (Northern Line)
Bus: 24, 27, 31, 168
Open: Monday-Saturday 8.30am-5pm

Not nearly as eclectic as the neighbouring conglomeration of Camden markets, Inverness Street has its own quiet allure with its colourful selection of fruit and veg. One of the last places in the area where you can do your daily shopping al fresco, it is well loved by locals and has been in operation since 1900. Fruit and veg and cut flowers are the mainstay of the street's stalls, but you can also find football jerseys, casualwear and tacky souvenirs. Progress cannot be halted and Virgin Megastore has installed a branch here. Inverness Street is a great place to escape the maddening crowds of the Camden markets and have a bite to eat or refreshing drink while taking care of the more mundane but rather necessary shopping.

Refreshment

There is a surprisingly good selection of eateries here. Bar Gansa, a Spanish establishment at no. 2, is a popular Inverness Street haunt where you can indulge in red wine and tapas. Bar Vinyl at no. 6 is an innovative record shop-cum-bar that stocks many of its own issue house music. DJs, of course, are part and parcel of the scene here. Bar Solo at no. 20 and Bar Uno at no. 4 are trendier haunts and ideal for a swish drink. For Asian bites, try Singapore Sling at no. 10.

Getting a Stall

For further details contact Camden Council (see appendix).

KILBURN SQUARE, NW6

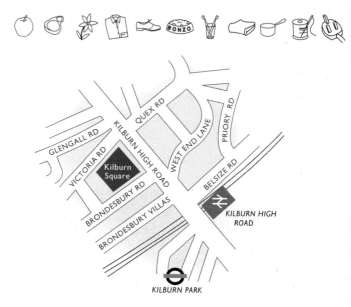

Kilburn High Road between Brondesbury Road & Victoria Road
Tube: Kilburn Park (Bakerloo)
Rail: Kilburn High Road
Bus: 16, 28, 32, 98, 189, 206, 316 (Kilburn High Road)
Open: Monday-Saturday 9am-5.30pm

Being stuck beneath an architectural tangle of access walkways that lead to the adjacent residential area and situated next to the grimiest stretch of NW London's arterial road, Kilburn Market (although fairly friendly) isn't the place to head for a pleasant potter. Inside the railings – the complex is a bit uninviting, despite the cheerful blue and yellow livery – a series of lock-up units stock a pretty average range of cheap goods, supplementing the functional selection on offer in the busy High Street. Here you can find fruit and veg, African groceries, new clothes, plants and flowers, household goods and toiletries, bedding and towels (the duvet plus pillowcase deals are worth a look), underwear, jewellery, hair accessories, hats, carpets, luggage, kids' clothes and electrical goods – in short, the sort of stuff you can get anywhere.

Although in general nothing here warrants a special trip, the market does hold pockets of interest in the form of a discount trainers stall and 'Rainbow Fabrics' – a haberdashery crammed full of glitzy fabrics (priced at between £1.50 and £3 a metre), whose owner maintains it is one of the few shops left which can give John Lewis a run for its money. The twin pet-care units, the One Step Shop and Paul's Aquatic World are both established businesses. If you ever doubted the market viability of consumer goods for gerbils, think again: One Step stocks a plethora of treats, homes, beds, toys and vanity products, without ignoring timeless favourites like the squeaky ball and novelty bone. Next door, Paul's houses wall to wall tanks, with an impressive range of both tropical and freshwater fish, with prices starting at £1 for a goldfish to £20 plus for more exotic types – a 'Discus', 'Silver Dollar' or 'Bumble Bee' can all be bagged up for you.

Refreshment

Decent refreshments are thin on the ground here, although Kabul John's in the far right hand corner of the market serves up standard greasy-spoon fare. The café is worth a visit if only for a look at the selection of posters on the wall where Sugar Ray Leonard and Roberto Duran vie for space with the Spice Girls. If you want to enjoy a coffee in a more conventional environment, try Caffè Nero which is just outside the market on the junction with Brondesbury Road. Further south opposite Kilburn High Road tube station are a number of reasonable caffs, including the very popular Ryans Diner.

Getting a Stall

The market is privately run by Hazeldean Properties, for further details contact the market manager on 01753 663 313 or 07768 206 754.

NAG'S HEAD, N7

a) Nag's Head Market
b) Grafton School Car Boot Sale

HOLLOWAY RD

South side of Seven Sisters Road at Holloway Road junction

Tube: Holloway Road (Piccadilly)

Bus: 4, 17, 29, 43, 91, 153, 259, 271, 279

Open: Monday, Tuesday, Thursday 9am-5pm (new and second-hand goods market); Wednesday 9am-3.30pm (second-hand and antiques market); Friday-Saturday 9am-5pm (new goods market), Sunday 7am-2pm (flea market)

Nestled behind the Nag's Head shopping market parking lot and with an entrance also on bustling Seven Sisters Road, this market of rickety stalls provides an indoor shopping venue most days of the week. The character of the market is much the same on a day-to-day basis, but the array of goods sold vary depending on when you visit.

In general, there are always plenty of stalls selling everyday necessities such as food, household goods, and new clothing. As well as the usual fruit and veg merchants there is also a fishmonger and a stall selling cut-rate brand name packaged food such as five full-size Snickers for £1.

Wednesday is the biggest day, but its official status as an antiques market is a slight misnomer. It's certainly more of a second-hand market with stall upon stall selling used clothing. Women are well catered for with racks of dresses and labels varying from designer to High Street brands to a few vintage party dresses; prices differ dramatically – from a few £1 racks to £30 for a silk Ghost dress. There are also a few stalls selling old records, vintage plates, and household accessories.

The Sunday flea market features more electronic goods and bric-à-brac than its Wednesday counterpart while Friday and Saturday see the stalls full of shiny, new goods for the home and body such as cheap cleaning supplies and inexpensive cotton underwear and pyjamas. Other useful stalls include a key cutter and a stall selling fabric for 50p a metre.

Refreshment

Jour et Nuit, a Moroccan bistro, at 316 Holloway Road is a pleasant place for a simple, strong coffee or a meal of lovely couscous dishes and tagines. For a different ethnic flavour, pull up a chair at El Molino at 379 Holloway Road for Spanish tapas. Both of these restaurant offers authentic fare for less than £20 a head – a welcome change from the usual pricey London dining out. For cheaper fare, step into one of the myriad fast food chains on the road. The bagel shop near the Clarks Factory Shop is rather good too.

Local Attractions

Seven Sisters Road accommodates plenty of merchants selling cheap, plastic household goods as well as halal butchers and cafés. Bargain hunters visiting the market might also want to check out Rolls and Rems fabric shop (21 Seven Sisters Road). Further down the road away from Holloway Road is the Clarks Factory Shop (67-83 Seven Sisters Road) where bargain shoes for the whole family can be found.

Getting a Stall

Call the market manager on tel: 020 7607 3527 or stop by his caravan at the rear of the market. Stalls are available from £14 per day.

QUEEN'S CRESCENT, NW5

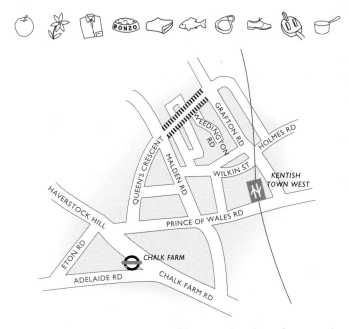

Queen's Crescent, between Malden Road and Grafton Road

Tube: *Kentish Town or Chalk Farm (Northern Line)*
Rail: *Kentish Town West*
Bus: *24,31, 27, 31, 168, 214 (Chalk Farm Road)*
Open: *Thursday 8.30am-2.30pm and*
Saturday (busiest day) 8.30am-4pm

Queen's Crescent is an anonymous street which is off the beaten track and easily missed. For this reason the market that takes place here on a Thursday and Saturday is a very local affair with people swapping gossip and news as they wander from stall to stall. The community is a mixture of Irish, Jamaican and Asian people, but the atmosphere is friendly and there is none of the tension witnessed at some of the larger markets.

north

Rival fruit and veg stalls mean some healthy bargains, and stock-piled bras, socks and undies all go for around a pound, while the plant stall has sophisticated greenery for under a tenner. Although unexciting, the other stalls are worth a look for good deals on new clothes, trainers, fish, meat, flowers, bedlinen, groceries, electrical goods, kitchen equipment, jewellery and even stationery. The leather stall was particularly good value with belts for £4.99, bags for £3.99 and purses for only £2. The bedding and towel stall was also offering some cracking deals with large bath towels for only £5. Just off the market on Malden Road is a very good junk shop which on a recent visit had an old wooden canoe for £70 and books for just 20p a go.

Queen's Crescent is not the sort of market you would go to for anything particularly original, and many of the stalls also trade from other markets during the week, but the local community atmosphere makes it a pleasant place to stoll and shop for basic essentials.

Refreshment
There are a few places to eat along the Crescent, but the best are the Blue Sea Fish Shop and the Gossip Stop Café which, with its lemon yellow walls, cheap fry-ups and Jam Roly Poly (£1), is a cheery place to work on the waistline. For alcohol there are two pubs at either end of the market, Man of Aran and Sir Robert Peel.

Local Attractions
Further north along Malden Road there are a few interesting junk shops which are worth a visit. At 94 Queen's Crescent the Ex-Catalogue Shop offers a good choice of domestic electrical goods most of which are greatly reduced slight seconds. The Kentish Town City Farm is also nearby in Cressfield Close for a temporary escape from city streets.

Getting a Stall
For further details contact Camden Council (see appendix).

SWISS COTTAGE, NW3

north

Between Avenue Road and Winchester Road

Tube: Swiss Cottage (Jubilee)
Rail: South Hampstead
Bus: 13, 46, 82, 113, 187, 268 (Avenue Road);
C11, C12, 31 (Adelaide Road)
Open: Friday, Saturday (busiest day) & Sunday 9.30am-4.30pm

Swiss Cottage market has a real community spirit and is one of the best things about this area dominated by large arterial roads. It is a testament to the local's commitment to the market that it has survived the ongoing re-development of the square undertaken by property developers in conjunction with Camden Council. The market has been on this site for over twenty years and although it has been moved to one side and enclosed by the boarding surrounding the building site it is still fighting on and the number of stalls has actually increased in recent months. There are plans for the market to move round the corner to Eaton Avenue by the spring of 2004, but the date of the move has been put back several times and it may be delayed again.

The market is best visited on a Saturday when about 20 stalls set up here under the shade of the square's remaining trees. The market still has a lot to offer the visitor with several good second-hand book dealers offering some great contemporary fiction including names like McEwan, Faulks and Amis as well as some reference and academic texts. One book trader combined his literary offerings with a well-chosen selection of classical CDs for just £2.50 each. The stall selling DVDs and videos is large, extending over four tables, and featuring anything from a Powell and Pressburger classic to Porkies 3. Sartorial bargains abound with designer label cast-offs going for outstanding prices, and plenty of cheap first-hand and occasional retro items; the jewellery is also good. There are several traders offering good condition kids' clothes with quality stuff from Osh Kosh and M&S and a more limited range of kids' toys. In keeping with the market's idealistic hippy origins in the 1970's, there is still a trader selling crystals and stone jewellery.

One of the best things about Swiss Cottage is the range of good bric-à-brac stalls that show up here on a Saturday. One stall was particularly interesting with a collection of three small French vases for only a fiver, an attractive set of old kitchen scales for £40, and some very fine linen table clothes for £3 each. A welcome addition to the market is the TV and video stall which has a reasonable selection of video recorders for just £25 and bargains such as a 21" Sony TV for just £90. The market also has a worthwhile fruit and veg stall which provides good quality essentials, but nothing unusual or exotic.

Refreshment

The Thai food stall is one of the market's major draws and brings in people from far afield. The food is freshly pepared and very good value with spicy treats for just £1 and a Thai curry with rice for only £3.50. The community centre has been moved to a temporary porta-cabin next door to the market, but still dishes up good value hot and cold food all week.

Local Attractions

The Freud Museum (20 Maresfield Gardens, tel: 020 7433 2002) is the nearest major attraction and is based at Freud's last home. The library next door to the market is well worth a look at for its period piece interior, it also houses one of London's best collections of psychology and philosophy books. Sadly, the excellent public swimming pool is closed during the building work.

Getting a Stall

The market is privately run (with profits funding charity projects). For further details contact Lindy on 07949 725 407 or e-mail: market@lovelyjubbly.co.uk.m

WEMBLEY SUNDAY MARKET, HA9

Car park between Olympic Way and First Way
(north side of Wembley Stadium)

Tube: Wembley Park (Metropolitan Line)

Rail: Wembley Stadium

Bus: 83, 92, 182, 204, 223, 297, PR2

Open: Sunday 9am-2pm

s a child, my father used to take me to Wembley Stadium
Market on a Sunday and buy me things like pens that write in
three different colours or cheap plastic Thunderbird toys. I was
always excited about going to the market and always disappointed when
the toy I had been campaigning for fell apart in my hands on the same
afternoon. Times have changed. Wembley's twin towers have been
reduced to rubble in preparation for the new stadium, and now I take

my own daughters to the market – although the kids' toys are as fragile as they have always been. The market is massive extending over a large car park and it has a kind of down-at-heel, fairground atmosphere with juddering generators, lively stallholders, good-humoured crowds, the smell of doughnuts and burgers, and the pulse of musical tasters from the CD stalls. It's still an exciting place to wander with the throng, but as with many Sunday car park markets (see Wimbledon Stadium page 142, and Nine Elms page 136) the experience lacks any charm and the goods are all new and mostly aimed at the budget shopper.

What Wembley Market does have in its favour is choice: if one fleece jacket isn't quite what you want, there are around thirty other stalls which can sell you an alternative. Clothes in general are better than average, with the High Street seconds/copies stalls offering good buys: 3 fashionable T-shirts for £10, or leather jackets from £40; plus there are plenty of more unusual examples of (predominantly girls') fashion separates at low-commitment prices, and towards the middle of the market, lots of shirts, jeans, jackets, sportswear, shoes and trainers.

As befits any down-to-earth market, utility goods make up the bulk of the merchandise. Tides of functional bedding, throws (some nice Moroccan-style sofa covers for £15), pillows, towels, dishcloths, cheap electronic items (miked-up 'auctioneers' are dotted throughout the market, trying to bait an audience with £1 stereos and threadbare banter), tools, bags, purses and dumpbins of miscellaneous 50p wonders wash all round the market. But slotted in amongst all this, the odd outcrop of idiosyncracy does manage to thrive, with a well-stocked stationery stall and even a milliner offering a good choice of ladies hats. A few cheap music stalls also buck the '101 Opera Anthems' trend of many local markets, doing a good line in both chart and back catalogue albums (mainly dance, swing and soul), with some providing decks for customers to try out the more obscure vinyl.

Wembley Stadium isn't one of the best places to visit for grocery shopping, but the few fruit and veg stalls are large concerns offering bargains like six nectarines for £1 and ten oranges for the same price. The several meat stalls scattered around the market likewise offer some great deals with meaty essentials like pork, beef and lamb all sold at well below High Street prices. Parking isn't cheap (around £6), so if you want to keep the money you have saved at the market you are better off sticking to public transport - the walk from Wembley Park tube is only five minutes.

Refreshment

There is an artery clogging selection of burger and doughnut stalls at Wembley Stadium Market. If you want something a little different there is a central eating area with stalls offering food from around the world, including several Indian food stalls serving fresh naan breads and spitting kebab sticks.

Getting a Stall

For further details about getting a stall contact Wendy Fair on 01895 632 221

WEST LONDON

Bayswater Road & Piccadilly   96

Hammersmith Road   99

King's Road Antiques   101

North End Road   103

Portobello   106

Shepherd's Bush   116

west

BAYSWATER ROAD & PICCADILLY, W2 & W1

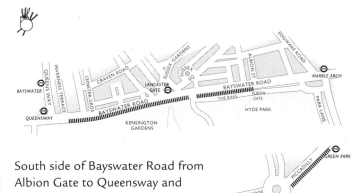

South side of Bayswater Road from
Albion Gate to Queensway and
south side of Piccadilly from
Queen's Walk to Hyde Park Corner

Tube: *Lancaster Gate, Marble Arch (Central),*
Green Park (Victoria, Piccadilly and Jubilee)
Bus: *8, 9, 14, 19, 22, 38 (Piccadilly); 12, 94, 148 (Bayswater)*
Open: *Sunday 9.30am-4pm (Piccadilly & Bayswater Road),*
Saturday 9.30am-4pm (Piccadilly)

These two art fairs are great place to stroll on a Sunday. Start at the
Piccadilly art fair then walk through Hyde Park to reach the
Bayswater fair. Serious art buyers will find few items of interest,
but for browsing the markets are great. It's almost like an outdoor art
gallery (if you can ignore the touristy souvenir stalls), but minus the
pretension and, unfortunately, occasionally minus the artistry.

Most of the artists are on hand to sell their paintings, and many of
them take credit cards. This is a sophisticated market, even though its
wares are aimed at tourists or those looking for stereotypical paintings. All
styles of painting are covered from Renaissance to pop art. One guy even
sells velvet canvases depicting roaring lions or sensuous female figures.

Tourists have a wealth of schlock from which to choose. Oxford
sweatshirts, London T-shirts and key rings and refrigerator magnets with

emblems of the capital abound. For teenagers on holiday, there are plenty of stalls at the Green Park station end of the Piccadilly market selling mass-produced silver and leather jewellery from Asia and bright coloured hairbands and beads. There are souvenirs that have nothing to do with London such as the turquoise scarab beetle figurines and papyrus prints at the Egyptian art stall. Even more curious is the stall selling "bulk art" where those on the move can pick up three paintings for £10. For smaller budgets, there are mini prints in wee frames with magnets on the back for just £1.50 each. These miniature paintings depict London scenes. Also at the Green Park station end of the Piccadilly market are pub towels, beer coasters and plenty of satirical prints about British life. Some might prefer paintings of flowers which plenty of the dealers stock. These are of the Victorian parlour variety complete with Latin name inscribed under the flowery subject. More souvenir-style paintings abound in the Piccadilly market with paintings depicting 19th-century London street scenes. For as many London scenes depicted there are an equal amount portraying the English countryside with subjects like canals, cows and generic countryside.

The many animal paintings (both oil and watercolour) range from elephants and lions to hens and horses. A significant number of artists devote themselves solely to portraying the different breeds of dogs and cats. Cityscapes (London to New York), seascapes (with plenty of tropical beach scenes) and landscapes (from battles to Turneresque renderings) are also offered. The only thing there isn't is an escape. However, if you need a map of London, a few Piccadilly vendors do sell these.

One of the oddest creations that are seen repeatedly at the market are clocks that are made using clock parts to represent famous landmarks. Big Ben is an obvious favourite for this unusual art form. Other oddities are the figurines made from kitchen utensils. These at least have a slightly avant-garde, whimsical look to them that might fit in with a modern décor. The clocks on the other hand are very kitsch.

Most of the vendors advertise in more than one language and will pack up paintings to be shipped abroad – more testament to the fact that this market is not for native Londoners. One vendor even gives away a free T-shirt with every print bought.

The Bayswater market is a little quieter, but no less amusing. There are plenty of portrait artists here depicting Native Americans, iconic Americans like Marilyn Monroe, Jimi Hendrix and Woody Allen and famous Brits like David Beckham. Landscapes here tend to be restricted to either Greek or Spanish villages, tropical beach scenes or romantic Renaissance-style paintings of women sleeping in groves, on balconies, under trees, etc. If you want something a little more personal, a caricaturist will draw a likeness of you. Another personal service is the artist who makes personalised birth announcements, wedding announcements or can paint your child's name onto a flowery, pastel background. There is slightly more modern art here with plenty of vibrant squares of colour and abstract paintings. Of course, there are also some weird pieces too such as the Disney characters painted on papyrus and the oil paintings of modern airline jets (British Airways, United, etc.) in the sky. Lichtenstein, Picasso and Andy Warhol rip-offs/homages are plentiful at the Bayswater market. Watercolours of London scenes go for £10. Giant oil paintings in the tradition of Old Masters can cost as much as £500.

Refreshment

From the north side of Piccadilly, (opposite the market) head down White Horse Street to Shepherd Market where there are plenty of cafés – some with outdoor seating. From the Bayswater market, head up Queensway to find some of London's best dim sum at Royal China no. 13 or Chinese seafood at Mandarin Kitchen at no. 14. Neither take Sunday reservations, so be prepared to wait.

Local Attractions

Hyde Park offers a plethora of adventures such as boating on the Serpentine, rollerblading through the park, having tea at the Orangery near Kensington Palace, checking out the Royal Dress Collection at Kensington Palace or just having a cuppa from one of the cafés while watching London go by.

Getting a Stall

For further details, contact Westminster City Council (see appendix).

HAMMERSMITH ROAD, W6

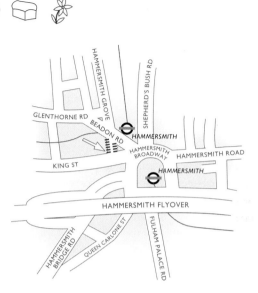

Hammersmith Grove, between King Street and Beadon Road
Tube: Hammersmith (Hammersmith & City, Piccadilly and District)
Bus: 9, 10, 27, 33, 72, 190, 209, 211, 220, 283, 295, 391
Open: Monday-Saturday 9am-5pm

Hammersmith Market has been struggling to survive for the last ten years and in the last two years the number of stalls has dwindled from seven to a meagre three offering fresh flowers, fruit and veg and good bread respectively. The three stalls do not always show up and on a busy Friday afternoon it is possible to find just the friendly fruit and veg man plying his trade – his only company being a lone fly-trader selling cheap jewellery from a blanket. John Tydeman's fish stall had been in the family for over 100 years, but he too has moved on, marking the end of an era and the gradual transition from a proper street market into an intermittent handful of stalls.

The decline of the market is a loss for this large open square given its proximity next to a cashpoint machine and to Hammersmith tube station. The problem is partly caused by the change in shopping habits with most people these days preferring to shop in the massive King's Mall in whose shadow the market now struggles on. If you should be passing have a look at the few old wooden stalls that can still be found here, these ancient wooden carts are the last remnant of the market's more illustrious past.

Refreshment
The lively, Formica-clad, Broadway Snack Bar has now closed, marking another regrettable change to the area. The nearest place to get a coffee is now the Pret à Manger on the corner.

Local Attractions
The florist on Beadon Street is still trading from its Victorian frontage and its flower-crammed windows are always worth a visit for those in search of flora.

Getting a Stall
For further details contact Hammersmith & Fulham Council (see appendix).

KING'S ROAD ANTIQUES (Antiquarius), SW3

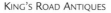

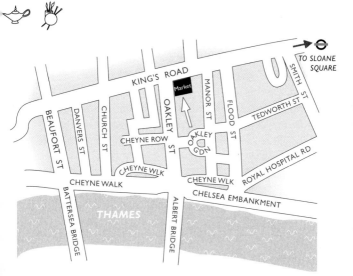

131-41 King's Road

Tube: South Kensington, Sloane Square (Circle Line)

Bus: 11, 19, 22, 49, 211, 319, 345

Open: Monday-Saturday 7.30am-6pm

The Antiquarius antiques market is a little difficult to spot from the street as the front units of the building have now been given over to smart boutiques which blend in with the other shops on the King's Road. Once through the entrance you are immediately made aware of how stylish this arcade is with antique dealers trading from glass fronted units that are more like shops than any kind of market stall. The grandeur of the upper level of Antiquarius is matched by the equally grand antiques for sale which are probably beyond the budget of most of us, but are still great to look at. The unit called Art-Deco Pavilion is a good example with its thick carpets and some very fine Art-Deco pieces, none of which carry a price label, giving the impression that those who want (or need) to discuss prices are not welcome.

The luxurious nature of the place does not extend to the lower level which is still very clean and pleasant, but which has lower ceilings and lino on the floor rather than stone. The quality of antiques and their asking prices are still high, with three large wooden Flemish saints selling for £3,500, and a specialist in glassware offering a set of eight Lalique glasses for £1,600. One of the units at the back of the lower hall had some more affordable pieces with an attractive chess set for £180 and even a small selection of second-hand books for just a few pounds each. My favourite stall was the one extending over two units which specialised in 20th century painting including a large William Leonard oil on canvas which was reasonable value for £550.

Antiquarius is a fascinating place to wander around and those without the budget to afford fine antiques can still while away a few hours using the place as a museum. The market is getting quieter though – traders say they are missing the American tourists who are not coming to London in such great numbers since 9/11, and trade has also been hit by a general decline in interest in antiques and collectables.

Refreshment

There are plenty of good cafés on King's Road, but the Antiquarius Café makes a mean cappuccino and offers wholesome meals for around a fiver.

NORTH END ROAD, SW6

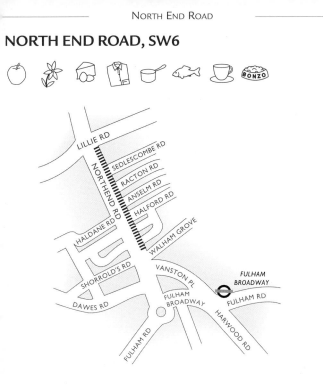

East side of North End Road, from Walham Grove to Lillie Road

Tube: Fulham Broadway (District)

Bus: 28, 391 (North End Road); 74, 190 (Lillie Road);
11, 14, 211, 295 (Fulham Broadway)

Open: (Main market) Monday-Saturday 7am-5pm, Thursday 7am-1pm
(Saturday busiest day)

Fulham is one of the smarter parts of London, but the area north west of Fulham Broadway forms a rectangle of pretty ordinary streets, slotted in amongst other, posher districts. The North End Road reflects the contrast, starting off relatively classy but becoming more and more scruffy as you walk northwards past run-down buildings and a string of £1 shops and cheap chain stores. There are signs that even this part of town is becoming smarter and one consequence of this has been the closure of the old Crowthers Market to be replaced by a housing development. Crowthers Market was a charming place to find second-hand and collectable things and its disappearance is a serious loss to the area.

North End Road is still a good market which attracts reasonable business during the week, but is at its most exciting on a Saturday when the full contingent of stalls extends along the east side of North End Road between Lillie Road and Waltham Grove. It services mainly everyday needs with an extensive array of goods from fruit and veg to carpets and pet-care accessories with the odd ultra-specialist stall such as the one selling Hoover bags. The man running the flower stall on the corner of Racton Road has been trading here for 58 years and is pessimistic about the market's future. He now does a second job in the evenings to make ends meet although he manages a smile and some advice for customers as they choose from his selection of cut flowers. Another long established favourite on the market is the fresh fish stall which offers good deals like Scotch salmon for £2.50 lb, sea bass for only £4.50 lb and a very impressive selection of smoked fish. The egg stall is also worth a look at with farm fresh eggs for only 65p a half-dozen and some unusual things like huge goose eggs which you won't find at any supermarket. The cheap perfume and cosmetics stall is still going strong with lots of lipsticks and mascara for £1 a go, and copies of brand name perfumes with names like 'Obvious' (Obsession) for £4 a bottle.

There are a few stalls selling cheap fashion clothing, underwear and small electrical goods but the fruit and veg stalls predominate on the street and attract the most customers, with a lot of casual as well as regular shoppers hooked in by impressive bargains, like 10 oranges for £1 and a couple of pounds of Coxes for the same price. The core range is fairly conservative although Mediterranean vegetables, and the occasional exotic fruit are dotted about. Some of the best fruit and veg stalls are found at the southern end of the street and still make the effort with old-fashioned displays of regimented pears and apples sitting pertly on pink tissue paper to help encourage punters.

Refreshment

For Middle-Eastern cuisine there is a good Lebanese restaurant (Al-Dar) which is just opposite the junction with Racton Road. Further south at number 348 is The Café Fish Bar which has been serving fish and chips here for over thirty years. If you fancy a pint try The Cock, which is a traditional public house at the southern end of the street. Vanston Place has several good Italian diners which offer comfort food in a friendly environment.

Local Attractions

North End Road has several good charity shops and a little further south is TNT, an excellent retro clothing shop which is well worth a visit for stylish clothing on a budget.

Getting a Stall

For further details contact Hammersmith & Fulham Council (see appendix).

PORTOBELLO. W11

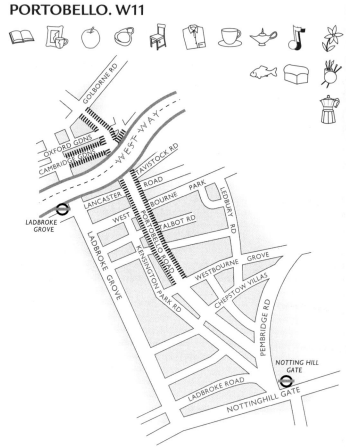

Portobello Road from (and including) Golborne Road to Chepstow Villas

Tube: Notting Hill Gate (Central, Circle or District), Ladbroke Grove (Hammersmith & City)

Bus: 7, 12, 23, 27, 28, 31, 52, 70, 94, 328

Open: Monday-Wednesday, Friday-Saturday 8am-6.30pm, Thursday 8am-1pm (general market), (Wednesday, and Friday 8am-6.30pm, Thursday 8am-1pm , Friday-Saturday 8am-6.30pm (antiques), Sunday 9am-1pm (Car Boot Sale), Mon-Sat 9am-5pm (Golborne Road)

"...the best and oddest market for antiques in London..." V.S. Pritchett

Shopping is possible here all week, but the southern end of Portobello Road near Notting Hill Gate is most famous for its Saturday antiques market with over 1500 street stalls and scores of shops. Antiques have been sold at the market since the 18th century. The weekday market stocks fruit and veg, household goods and clothing. The food is fresh and there is a good range of exotic produce catering for the local West Indian, North African and Portuguese communities. From Friday to Sunday second-hand clothes and bric-à-brac can be found under the Westway.

The Saturday Antiques Market begins at 5.30am when the professional dealers trade. By 10am, the market is in full swing. The best selection is only available before lunch as some dealers close up then, but most stay until the end of the day.

Notting Hill has a diverse mix of residents hailing from all corners of the globe. Similarly, the market attracts a variety of nationalities to its streets. Asians, Europeans and Americans all congregate to browse and buy – after all the market is chock full of the biggest selection of antiques in Britain. In general, the quality control here is very tight so you do get what you pay for. Bargaining is always worth trying, particularly on the quieter days when the traders will compromise on price to boost their takings. Over 1500 dealers trade in the Saturday Antiques Market. Weekdays attract a neighbourhood crowd of West Indians, hippies, chic trust-fund beneficiaries, and young families who are out to do their daily shopping. Notting Hill is one of the richest and most fashionable parts of London, but it bares no resemblance to the eponymous Hollywood film staring Hugh Grant. With this in mind, you should always hold on to your belongings tightly when walking through the market as you are more likely to be rubbing shoulders with a pickpocket than a lovable English gent.

Whether you are shopping for retro duds, a ripe mango, a new broom or an antique clock, Portobello Road will deliver. The fashions here range from vintage to second-hand modern clothing to designer one-offs. Household goods cover the gamut from bin liners to light bulbs. You could easily do your weekly shopping here and find a plethora of exceptionally fresh produce..

The southern end of the market definitely caters to a more upmarket crowd with its genuine antiques and as the mile-long road winds its way north, the goods become more modern, less posh and, perhaps, more interesting. If you're looking for the next big fashion trend, the northern end is a good place to start searching as many young designers hawk their creative wares here.

Portobello Market extends for well over a mile and can be very roughly divided into three parts. The antiques section on the southern end of the street nearest to Notting Hill Gate is the most famous and best-loved part. The general fruit and veg market is in the central part of Portobello Road and is a great place to stock up on groceries. The flea market selling retro fashion and junk runs from the Westway to some way along Golborne Road and is the best territory for bargain hunters to explore.

Visiting the market on a Saturday should be reserved for those who have no fear of crowds and a great love of antiques. You should start at the Notting Hill Gate end of Portobello Road and make your way north with a plan to spend the better part of the day here. Notting Hill Gate tube confronts one with crowds of people and a few High Street chain shops. However, as soon as you turn and start walking down Pembridge Road to Portobello Road, you'll find charming little shops as well as some delightful pastel-coloured residences on your way to the market proper.

On other days, the crowds are not as crushing and the selection of stalls appeals to a more diverse audience. The weekday general market runs between Lonsdale Road and Lancaster Road. If you visit on a Saturday, but want to skip the antiques approach the market from Ladbroke Grove tube – you will have less of a crowd to fight against.

Chepstow Villas to Lonsdale Road
(antiques and collectables)

This is the genteel end of the market and is best approached from Notting Hill Gate. The true beginning of the market is at the intersection with Chepstow Villas. If you don't mind the crowds and want the best selection of goods, come on Saturday when stalls line the streets.

Of course, wintry days thin out the crowds, but not enough to make much of a difference. There is a reason this is one of the best antique markets in the world. The little touches like aged antique dealers who are experts on their stock, classical musicians busking, and a cacophony of languages make this a unique and memorable shopping trip.

On weekdays, the place is definitely more low-key and offers plenty of proper antique shops complete with helpful, knowledgeable staff. For goods a little more contemporary, check out the relatively new arts and crafts section showcasing artisans and their unique wares just off Portobello Road on the Tavistock Piazza. When it comes to goods for sale, the selection is outstanding. The basics are here – silverware, crystal, art nouveau jewellery, grandfather clocks and plenty of objets d'art. You can also find items specific to Britain such as Toby jugs, bargeware and china from UK manufacturers. These stalls are not run by amateurs, which means the quality of the goods and the calibre of the service are very high. The Chelsea Galleries (stall enquiries: 0207 376 4585) at no. 67, 69, and 73 offers plenty of stalls under cover. For desk items and scales try Kay Ramm. For 1920's toys, Rosslyn Neave is the place to look and for Victorian tea sets, stop by Yolanda. There are plenty of other dealers selling porcelain, glass, silver and jewellery in this little mall. Madge's Cafe is upstairs here and serves the usual British food such as gut-busting English breakfasts, satisfying lunches and teas.

Where Portobello meets Westbourne Road, the Good Fairy Antique Market runs about 50 stalls (stall enquiries: 01634 233900) where jewellery, accessories, and silver are all good buys. Across the road is Roger's Antiques Gallery (stall enquiries: (020 7351 5353) with over 80 dealers. Roger's was the first indoor market on Portobello Road to sell antiques. In the midst of these well-stocked indoor markets, there are outdoor stalls selling all manner of goods from beautiful vintage lace and silver service to modern-day plastic bric-à-brac. Farther along is the Admiral Vernon Antique Market at no. 141 (stall enquiries: 020 7727 5242) where there is a café as well as hundreds of dealers. Lonsdale Road is basically the finishing point for the antiques traders even though a few lie beyond this point.

west

Lonsdale Road to Lancaster Road
(Food, flowers and clothing)

This portion of the market is much more ordinary selling many mass-produced everyday items such as cheap clothing, fresh food and cut flowers. The Duke of Wellington at no. 179 marks the beginning of the food section and is a pleasant place for a pint. Walking north on Portobello, you'll encounter olives, fresh breads and plenty of fruit and veg. Nods to North African roots are apparent in the dried fruit and nuts stands, tropical fruits piled high and interesting spices available. The choice of European breads at the Breadstall, no. 172, is tantalising. During the week, the choice is limited to everyday food and drink items, and on Saturdays, the selection expands to include plenty of hot food stalls selling Jamaican, Thai and even German food. Just off Portobello Road, Blenheim Crescent offers plenty of opportunity for inspiration. At no. 13, the Travel Bookshop sells guidebooks, coffee table books and plenty of travel literature. At no. 11, Garden Books caters to garden enthusiasts. Books for Cooks across the street at no. 14 is a mecca for culinary artistes, and features cookbooks, cooking classes and a wonderful eatery in the rear serving inexpensive gourmet treats. After Books for Cooks, the Spice Shop at no. 1 is a perfect stop to pick up hard-to-find herbs and spices. This part of the market can be enjoyed any day of the week and if you come on Thursday, there's the added bonus of organic foods such as grains, dried fruits, speciality breads and fruit and veg.

Lancaster Road to the Westway
(New Clothing and household goods)

Here the market concentrates on the kind of new clothes and household goods to be found at most local markets. The goods are not very inspirational but there are enough good quality designer copies to make the area worth a gander. Handbags, watches, fabric, scarves and trainers are all up for grabs along this portion of the market. Occasionally, you might just find something of interest amid the dross. The shops behind the stalls are mix of hippy wares and products for hip clubbers.

west

west

Under the Westway and west up to Ladbroke Grove
(Retro and new clothing, CDs and records, books and collectables)
The flyover that is the Westway marks the beginning of a funkier and more entertaining part of the market. This is a glimpse of Notting Hill before the gentrification and before the media hype changed the area beyond recognition. The second-hand garments here are inspiring for retro dressers and there are numerous young designers selling unique handmade items from their stalls. Of course, the selection of bric-à-brac supports this area of the market's reputation as the seedier, more down-at-the-heels end. The Portobello Green Market (stall enquiries: 020 8962 5724) sits snugly next to the flyover on Thorpe Close and sells all manner of hip designer goods that are exclusively found here. The feeling is a bit more upmarket here and definitely less crowded so it's a good place to indulge in a spot of caffeine in the premises' café. Along the street, be on the lookout for 50s' party dresses, 70s' interior design accessories as well as Art Deco and 1950s and 60s memorabilia.

Portobello Road from Acklam Road to Golborne Road
(Retro and new clothing, bric-à-brac, furniture, household and electrical goods)
This is serious bargain hunting territory. Most stalls are more like jumble sales than their southern neighbours where things are bit better presented. Still the organisational skills of the stallholders dictate the price – the better the presentation; the higher the prices. Still shoppers on a budget with a keen eye and plenty of enthusiasm may do their best shopping along this section of the market. There are lots of bargains to be found here with a pair of brand new running trainers for only £10, a set of good quality pans for £12 the set and one trader offering a well selected and presented selection of quality second-hand clothes with jeans for as little as £4 a pair.

west

Golborne Road Market
(Junk, furniture and fruit and veg)

Running from Portobello Road to St Ervans Road, Golborne Road market is at the heart of Moroccan and Portuguese London and marks the end of the Portobello Market area. It's best approached from the Ladbroke Grove station. In recent years, the market has gone more upscale than it once was, but it still has an authentic ethnic feel to it. The main change has been the increase of high-end antique shops selling beautiful items for the home. This a great place to escape the tourist while enjoying a bit of the Portobello Road experience in a diverse environment. On weekdays, fruit and veg traders hawk their wonderfully fresh, delicious and sometimes exotic produce. There are also all the other requisite general market stalls from household goods like bin liners and mops to hot food for shopping sustenance. Fridays and Saturdays see an onslaught of more traders who deal mainly in bric-à-brac and second-hand goods creating a delightful riot of jumbled goods for sale. In keeping with the multicultural feel, the food here is not British. One of the best places for a nosh is Lisboa Patisserie at no. 57 serving delightful Portuguese pastries and strong coffee. Of interest to architecture enthusiasts will be the soaring Trellick Tower that hovers over the skyline here. It was designed by Erno Goldfinger in 1973 and recently came under the protection of English Heritage with a Grade-II listed status.

Refreshment

Escape to Lisboa Patisserie at 57 Golborne road for a taste of its well-known Portuguese pastries such as custard tarts. Sausage & Mash at 268 Portobello Road under the Westway offers lip-smacking plates of sausages prepared in a variety of ways – with mash, as a sandwich or on their own. Vegetarians even get a choice of sausages. The Tea and Coffee Plant sells just what it advertises from its stall and shop at 170 Portobello Road. It sets itself apart from the competition such as Starbuck's, which also occupies premises on the road, by roasting and grinding its own beans. Plenty of healthy and tasty teas too. Books for Cooks on Blenheim Crescent serves lunches in the back of their shop. Of course, the most adventurous way to eat here is from one of the hot food stalls. The German Brautwurst stall is particularly good.

Shopping around the area

Boutiques line the streets around the market. Try Ledbury Road at Westbourne Grove, Clarendon Cross and Kensington Park Road for more high-end antiques shopping as well as trendy designer fashions for the home and body.

All Saints Road between Tavistock Road and is host to the area's concentration of music shops. Portobello Music at no. 13 also sells instruments and sheet music. A few fashionable women's clothing stores such as The Jacksons at no. 5 are here as well as a bicycle repair shop at no. 27 with a very good staff. This makes a pleasant commercial diversion from the hubbub of Portobello Road.

Festivals

Perhaps the area is most famous for its Notting Hill Carnival over the last bank holiday weekend in August. On that weekend, the market transforms (as do most other streets in the neighbourhood) into a seething, gyrating mass of humanity intent on shaking their bodies to the Afro-Caribbean tunes. For details, www.nhct.org.uk.

Getting a stall

There are two bodies responsible for running market stalls in Portobello:

a) Most of the market is run by Kensington & Chelsea Council (see Appendix)

b) Country Wide operate the stalls under the canopy and along the Westway, for further details phone 0800 358 3434.

west

SHEPHERD'S BUSH ,W12

Between Uxbridge Road and Goldhawk Road W12

Tube: Shepherd's Bush, Goldhawk Road (Metropolitan)
Bus: 49, 72, 94, 95, 207, 220, 237, 260, 272, 607, 283 (Uxbridge Road)
Open: Monday-Saturday 9am-5pm, Thursday 9am-1pm

Shepherd's Bush is a remarkably mixed area. On Shepherd's Bush Green there are large pubs packed with young people drinking too much beer and watching sport while just down Goldhawk Road at the entrance to Shepherd's Bush Market, Middle-Eastern women in full Islamic dress await the arrival of their limousines to take them home. It struck me as strange that women shopping at the local market should have a limousine, but it emerged that the limos are in fact glorified taxis that turn up every ten minutes to pick up their fares.

Entering the market from Goldhawk Road it is evident that the cultural mix is even more complex with many African, Middle-Eastern, West Indian and Asian people living, shopping and trading in the area. The market also has a variety of shops, lock-ups and stalls all vying for your attention as they extend parallel to the overhead Metropolitan line with the occasional sight of a tube train to remind you that this is still London and not some foreign bazaar.

The market does not just run along the eastern side of the tube line, but also has a fairly large square and a passageway on the western side which connects to the main market via two narrow arches. It is in this smaller maze of shops that most of the specialist African food stalls are situated as well as a few selling African music along with the usual mix of street fashion, cheap shoes, bags and a few outlets selling fabric by the yard. Among some of the more interesting outlets is the excellent Footsie 101 which offers fashionable footwear at below High Street prices. Dave's Drapers is another established feature of the market selling great value fabrics for as little as £1 per metre.

west

The market is especially strong on fresh food, with many top-notch fruit and veg stalls ranging from those dealing in standard fare to others with more exotic produce. One such stall is located about half-way down the market and has all kinds of unusual vegetables – yams, cassava, plantain and dried pumpkin. There are also several good butchers within the market selling basics as well as more recherché things to cater for the African community such as pigs trotters and cows' tongues. Likewise there are plenty of good fresh fish stalls offering anything from smoked haddock to fresh tuna and red snapper.

Although many of the things found at Shepherd's Bush Market are unexceptional, the atmosphere and diversity of the place make it worth visiting. There are also some real bargains to be found here – I recently came across a clothing stall selling well made Schott jackets for only £9.99 and some quality kitchenware including large aluminium pans for just £12.

Refreshment
There are several good falafel stalls along the market which reflect the culinary tastes of the Middle-Eastern locals. If you want traditional British food try A. Cooke pie and mash shop on Goldhawk Road.

Getting a Stall
The market is run by London Transport and there are all kinds of pitches available, for more details phone 020 7918 4067.

Southwest London

Battersea High Street 120

Brixton Market 122

Broadway and Tooting 127

Hildreth Street 130

Merton Abbey Mills 132

Nine Elms Sunday Market 136

Northcote Road 138

Wimbledon Stadium 142

southwest

BATTERSEA HIGH STREET, SW11

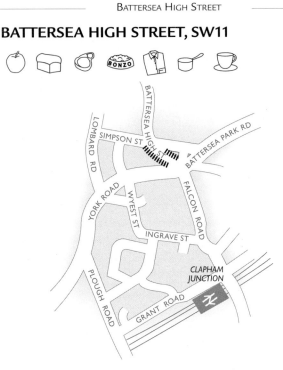

South end of Battersea High Street, up to the junction with Simpson Road

Rail: Clapham Junction (Victoria, Waterloo)

Bus: 44, 49, 319, 344, 345

Open: Friday-Saturday 9.30am-4.30pm

In its Victorian heyday this market was a huge and vibrant affair, and it was still running throughout the week twenty years ago, but now it is limited to two days a week and, as one stall-holder confessed, is only really busy on a Saturday. The market is located in a small pedestrian passageway backing onto a scruffy residential area in the heart of what estate agents would probably call the 'wrong' side of Battersea. It certainly isn't the place to find SW11 trendies doing some picturesque pottering: if you want that kind of experience head south to Northcote

Road Market (see page 138). There are signs however that the area is becoming smarter with the recent arrival of a trendy bar at the far end of the road and a new deli to cater for the better heeled foodie.

The market has not changed much in recent years and continues to supply basic goods to local people. It now only has six regular stalls which stick to the standards. The two large fruit and veg stalls are particularly good value with offers like 6lb of bananas for only £2 and 10 sweetcorn for the same price. The most exotic things they had on offer were mangoes, two of which could be bought here for £1. Other stalls include a large card stall, a pet food and accessories stall (with an extensive and grisly selection of pigs' extremities from 60p), and stalls selling biscuits, packet food and sweets, household goods, street clothes, socks and underwear, and flowers. The regular bread stall is popular with the locals providing anything from chiabatta to a traditional crusty white loaf. If you fancy getting your Sunday joint off the side of a lorry, then see what's on offer from the wholesale meat van at the end of the street, he has some good deals including large family packs of bacon for only £5.

southwest

Refreshment

Jack Hall Dining Rooms is a defiantly old fashioned caff which still serves a good cup of tea and offers traditional grub like Spotted Dick and Treacle Pudding. Another trusty favourite is Notarianni & Sons Italian Restaurant, with its particularly impressive Deco-style chrome-wrapped frontage. For a more contemporary dining experience try Chez Manny, a recent arrival at the far end of the street.

Local Attractions

This area doesn't have a great deal to offer the casual passer-by but there is a good charity shop at the top of the road and the Galapagos Deli is also worth a visit for more fancy foodstuffs.

Getting a Stall

For further details contact Wandsworth Council (see appendix).

BRIXTON MARKET, SW9

a) Brixton Village
b) Market Row
c) Reliance Arcade
d) Tunstall Road (Arts & Crafts)

southwest

Brixton Station Road, Pope's Road, Atlantic Road,
Electric Road and Electric Avenue

Tube/Rail: Brixton (Victoria and Northern Line)
Bus: 35, 37, 109, 118, 196, 250, 355, P4
Open: Monday-Saturday 8am-5.30pm, Wednesday 8am-1pm
Tunstall Road (arts & crafts) Saturday 9am-5pm
Brixton Village also Sunday 10am-4pm

Brixton was a rather smart place in the last century and there are still signs of its Edwardian grandeur in some of the architecture, particularly along Electric Avenue (which was one of the first streets to have electricity in the 1870's). The area was in decline for many years but took on a new lease of life when West Indians settled here after the war. Brixton market is now the best weekday market south of the river and a great place to visit if you're looking for fresh and exotic food, Indian fabrics and there are even some good second-

122

hand stalls for those in search of bargains. The market is a sprawling affair consisting of several roads, arcades and railway arches which can be a bit disorientating, but there are plenty of watering holes for those who need to stop and get their bearings.

Electric Avenue

This is one of the main thoroughfares of the market and a great place to start if your interest is food shopping. There are lots of excellent fruit and veg stalls here, as well as a top-notch fishmonger and butcher to complement the market. There's also a very good Thai supermarket near the junction with Atlantic Road, emphasising Brixton's cultural and culinary diversity. Food isn't the only thing on offer here and the number of stalls selling consumer durables like street fashion, jewellery, bedding and towels, fabric by the yard, household goods, bags, accessories and watches has increased in the last few years. Among the best deals were stylish men's cotton shirts for only £3.99, and anonymous brand jeans for £8 a pair. It's worth raising your eyes from the market to take notice of the rather grand Edwardian architecture that curves above the functional shop fronts, giving some a clue to Brixton's past prosperity.

Pope's Road

This small road leads on from Electric Avenue, but has none of that street's charm. In place of Edwardian architecture there are modern lock-ups lurking amid railway arches and an ugly Iceland supermarket. Making up for the environment are some fine fruit and veg stalls and quite a few stalls selling cheap fashion clothing and shoes, kids' clothing, small electrical goods, cut-price perfume and one specialising in net curtains. One of the entrances to Brixton Village is on Pope's Road, or alternatively you can continue on to Brixton Station Road.

Brixton Station Road

This part of Brixton used to be renowned for the number and diversity of its second-hand stalls. The numbers have dwindled in recent years and now just two stalls and two permanent lock-ups, centred around the

southwest

southwest

junction with Pope's Road, are all that remain. Only four years ago the upper part of Brixton Station Road had regular stalls and a caff, but this end is now empty. The place is still worth visiting and the two regular stalls are large and well-stocked with all kinds of second-hand and retro clothing and shoes. Bargains to be found here recently included hardly worn branded trainers from £10, a stylish selection of women's designer shoes for only a fiver and a fashionable Jaegar jacket for £8.

The two lock-ups that stand either side of Pope's Road, likewise offer a large stock of well-priced retro clothing. One of the outlets has diversified with old vinyl, videos, lamps and furniture scattered among the rails of clothing. At the entrance a pile of neatly folded cotton sheets were only £2 each. On the corner of Brixton Road there are a handful of stalls offering a mix of CDs, street fashion and a Chinese-run stall offering a good selection of oriental bags, kids' shoes and colourful jewellery. This is still a great part of the market to visit, but without some support from the council its future does not look certain.

Refreshment
There are some good places to eat on Brixton Station Road, the best being Jacaranda Garden and the Portuguese Max Snack Bar. There are also several kiosks serving Caribbean food.

Brixton Village (formerly Granville Arcade)
Although this is the largest arcade in Brixton Market it's surprisingly bright and airy with plenty of skylights and light-coloured walls. There are quite a few stalls stocking household goods, but this is a particularly good place to find exotic foods with many stalls selling Afro-Caribbean spices and flavourings, several good fishmongers and greengrocers as well as stalls specialising in Chinese and Asian ingredients. Although the main avenue is busy, the rest of the place is empty of people, with lots of vacant units among the handful of struggling traders. The management are currently embarking on a restoration of this part of the market and they have introduced Sunday opening, but it's too late for the aquarium unit which is planning to shut.

southwest

125

Refreshment

There are several good places to eat within the market, including the excellent Food Coffee Shack which has outdoor seating, and La Cuchara – an authentic Latin café.

Market Row

This indoor passageway between Atlantic Road and Electric Lane is as pleasantly light as Brixton Village. It has a reasonable selection of fruit and veg, street fashion, fresh fish, household goods and toiletries. Dombey Wholesale Butchers is one of the major attractions of the market and usually has a queue of people after a meaty bargain.

Refreshment

Market Row has lost a few of its notable eateries, but the stylish and good value pizzeria/café called Eco is still doing brisk business. For food without olive oil drizzled on it, try Ergan's for basic British fare.

Reliance Arcade

This narrow passageway is darker than the other arcades in the market and has only a handful of stalls offering kid's clothes and Christian iconography as well as being home to an excellent music outlet.

Tunstall Road (Arts & Crafts Market)

This recently created market has about ten regular stalls offering a mix of music CDs, new clothing, jewellery and flowers. The market is crammed into a small side street just off Brixton Road, and gets a lot of passing trade being just next door to Body Shop.

Getting a Stall

For further details contact Brixton Market Office on 020 7926 2530 between 8.30am and 4.30pm.

BROADWAY & TOOTING, SW17

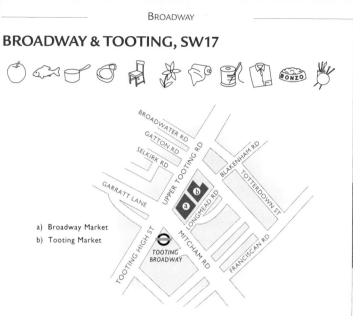

a) Broadway Market
b) Tooting Market

BROADWAY

Upper Tooting Road

Tube: *Tooting Broadway (Northern)*
Bus: *44, 77, 270, G1 (Garratt Lane);*
127, 133, 155, 219, 355, 264, 355 (Upper Tooting Road)
Open: *Monday-Saturday 9.30am-5pm, Wednesday until 1pm*

This covered market doesn't promise much from the street (the entrance nearest the tube is a gap between tacky shops leading into a dingy passage), but Broadway Market is certainly worth a look. The lack of steady trade and a tendency towards half-hearted presentation make it a bit underwhelming in terms of atmosphere, but the mixture of standard utility goods and services aimed at local Afro-Caribbean and Asian communities means there are plenty of cheap and interesting things to buy if you take time to explore its main "square" and access passageways (two lead off Upper Tooting Road).

southwest

Afro-Caribbean food and vegetables are well-stocked and supplemented by meat, seafood and fish stalls which all put impressively low prices on a wide range of stock, such as £9.99 for a big glistening salmon. There is also an excellent fruit and veg stall at the very back of the market, which has people queuing up enthusiastically for bargains like 2lbs of spinach for £1. The rest of the standard units offer lots of choice on household goods, stationery, underwear (including the exotic: £29.99 for an adult-sized nurse's uniform in lycra!), luggage and cosmetics, as well as the odd idiosyncrasy: the pasta-cum-artificial flower stall is a bit of a one-off. Fabric, haberdashery, Indian jewellery and accessories also get units to themselves so, for keen dressmakers, there's the possibility of knocking up endless ritzy outfits on the cheap. Other than the unit selling colourful kids' separates in the main square, the clothes on offer are pretty forgettable.

In amongst all this are specialist traders selling more unusual goods like African wood crafts, African batik and novelty balloons: order a while-you-wait balloon-twist giraffe for 50p. Broadway Market's nail salon can send you all Beverley Hills with glued on individual diamanté stars at 50p. The other unit worth a look is the fish and pet stall, which has tanks set up like an aquatic video wall, plus an impressive selection of kitschy fish accessories, plastic pond plants and general pet supplies.

Refreshment

Tooting Broadway is a bit of a café-free zone but the market's slightly dreary diner doesn't seem to be doing much to capitalise. It's probably best to fill up on something from the small Afro-Caribbean take-away (a plate of plantain and beans is £2.50) or go next door to Tooting Market which has a much more lively café. There is also Harrington's pie and mash shop, just across the way on Selkirk Road. Tooting is also a good place for a curry, with Lahore Karahi (1 Tooting High Street) being one of the best.

Getting a Stall

For further details contact the Market Office on 020 8672 6613.

TOOTING
Upper Tooting Road

Tube: *Tooting Broadway (Northern)*
Bus: *44, 77, 155, 270, 280, G1 (Garratt Lane);*
127, 133, 155, 219, 264, 355 (Upper Tooting Road)
Open: *Monday-Saturday 9.30am-5pm, Wednesday until 1pm*

A few yards further up Upper Tooting Road from Broadway Market is Tooting Market, it's slightly smaller but livelier twin. Essentially this L-shaped covered market covers the same sort of territory, with a range of utilitarian units enlivened by the odd unexpected specialist. Again, meat, fruit and veg are well covered, but the fish stall at the market's left-hand exit looks particularly impressive with some very fancy varieties on display: baby sharks go for 99p a pound, and a huge bag of live mussels is just £2.50.

The Afro-Caribbean influence is strong, with a large grocery shop in the far corner selling endless varieties of exotic vegetables. The Vallo Oriental Shop makes the choice of food even more international with a shop unit crammed full of what looks like every imaginable noodle and cooking sauce, as well as a great selection of herbs, teas (good quality oolong and jasmine leaf tea are cheap) and unusual canned beans and vegetables at well below supermarket prices.

In amongst the remainder of the stalls (standard market clobber and a cluster of traders flogging naff reproduction furniture and paintings), there are a few other noteworthy units: The Trimming Centre does a massive selection of embellishments for clothes and furnishings, and a watch stall doubles up by selling a wide range of vivid Vietnamese satin dresses, shirts and slippers in both adult and child sizes (£40 for a full length Suzi Wong-style dress). The old fashioned tobacconist is located at the Upper Tooting Road entance and sells all kinds of rare tobacco, pipes and other smoking paraphernalia.

Getting a Stall

The stalls are all permanent. If you're interested ask for an application form from the tobacconist at the entrance to the market, from where the market is run.

southwest

HILDRETH STREET, SW12

Hildreth Street

Tube: Balham (Northern)
Rail: Balham
Bus: 155, 249, 315, 355 (Balham High Road)
Open: Monday-Saturday 9.30am-5pm, Wednesdays until 1pm

Hildreth Street market has been located in this pedestrianised corridor between grand Toblerone-roofed Victorian buildings since the turn of the century, but is now a shadow of its former self with less than a dozen stalls. Despite its slightly neglected atmosphere, this small provisions market seems to be surviving well in the shadow of big hitters Safeway's and Sainsbury's who fight it out on either side of the High Road.

Hildreth Street market acts mainly as a supplement to a row of shops aimed at meeting the needs of Balham's Afro-Caribbean community. A choice of grocery units means that it's a good place to stock up cheaply on things like pulses, herbs, spices and more adventurous vegetables and you can get specialist breads or patties from the busy bakery.

There's an excellent range of fish on offer in the street, with exotic varieties such as yellow croaker available alongside more standard options, in either of the two fishmongers. The butchers is also a long established and popular local outlet which is a good value complement to the market's fruit and veg traders.

You're not going to find anything too exciting on the stalls themselves, but as a whole the market does a good job of providing cheap food to a steady flow of local shoppers. One stall sells tropical fruit (limes and mangoes are well priced) while the rest specialise in conventional British fruit and veg. Although these four stalls have nothing particularly flash on offer, the range of combined stock is quite impressive, with more unusual indigenous varieties of apples and old-fashioned berries stacked alongside lots of feisty-looking greens. The rest of the market is made up of stalls selling utility classics: eggs, cards, socks and underwear, as well as a small flower stall offering a reasonable selection of blooms.

southwest

Refreshment

Sadly Dot's, the oldest and most authentic caff in the area, has now closed. Balham Café on Hildreth Street is the closest substitute and Smileys on Bedford Hill is also a good basic caff. If you're after a decent coffee, try the branch of Caffé Nero just around the corner on Balham High Road.

Local Attractions

This area doesn't have too much to recommend it, but Etienne's is a well-stocked junk shop, just around the corner on Bedford Hill.

Getting a Stall

For further details contact Wandsworth Council (see appendix).

MERTON ABBEY MILLS, SW19

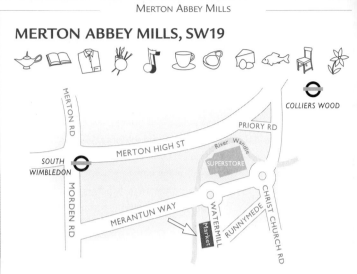

Off Merantun Way, Behind the Savacentre, South Wimbledon
Tube: Colliers Wood (Northern)
Bus: 57, 152, 200, 219
Open: Saturday-Sunday 10am-5pm,
Thursday 6am-12pm (antiques and collectables)

There are changes taking place at Merton Abbey Mills with the development of housing and a sports centre on the wasteland next to the mill, which was formerly used for parking. The development has lead to some resentment among traders at the market, particularly concerning the allocation of only 150 parking spaces for the whole site. Certainly the building works do not add to the charm of the place, but when the dust settles there is hope that the market will regain some of its composure. The development only really encroaches on the outer borders of the site and so the main body of the market, including the 18th century Watermill and Colourhouse, is largely unaffected by the works. The buildings were originally workshops used by artisans working in William Morris's Arts and Crafts style, but fell into disuse and dereliction after the war, only being restored and turned into a retail location in 1989.

southwest

132

The market itself is best visited on Sundays when over one hundred stalls set up here. It's a good place to find new clothes with a fair mix of fashion, smart casual and kidswear, but there are perhaps a few too many stalls selling tie dye hippie stuff for most people's liking. The best clothing stalls are located in the narrow passageway running alongside the indoor market. Here there is a very good stall selling men's smart casual clothing mostly bearing the Lambretta label with prices ranging from £15 for a short sleeve shirt to £28 for a fashionable denim jacket. Further along is the very popular women's fashion stall, offering slight seconds and samples with silk dresses starting from £10 and a well-stocked rail of garments reduced to clear for only £3. The regular customers seem to know a bargain when they see one with many of them buying armfuls of clothing rather than single items.

One of the most positive changes to the market in recent years is the addition of a selection of fine food stalls. This aspect of the market is organised by Keith Cook who also runs a top quality food stall sourcing fine foods from around the country including Scottish beef, farm fresh sausages and a delicious range of meats and cheeses from Denhay Farm in Dorset. Another important trader in this part of the market is Ron the fishman who sells a selection of very fresh fish, some of which he smokes on site. Both stalls trade from Friday to Sunday and have a loyal customer base who often order food in advance and simply pop by to collect their order. Other food stalls include one specialising in a wide selection of dried fruits and nuts, a farm stall selling fresh eggs and a selection of different apple juices and another offering prepared curry sauces and chutneys.

The indoor market (known as the Long Shop) has some excellent craft stalls with anything from a large leather sofa for £995 to hand-painted gift cards for just a few quid. There are quite a few artists selling their work, my favourite being large and vibrant oil paintings of flowers for between £95-£160. Another interesting stall stocked funky glass jewellery with colourful rings starting from £9. As with the clothes, it's very much a case of sorting the wheat from the chaff, with a great deal of novelty rubbish like the stall selling candles in the form of a naked woman with unfeasibly large breasts (an offence to good taste and a waste of wax to my mind).

southwest

southwest

One of the best things about the market is the number of good shops that have a permanent location here. It's particularly strong on second-hand books with several established bookshops on the site offering anything from expensive first editions to comics, and all of them extending their stock onto the pavement on market days. Thommo's is a large flower shop which also extends its stock onto the pavement at the weekend and offers a wide choice of cut flowers and plotted plants. For gifts, herbs and other craft items, the long established Greencades stands out as the best shop on site and has enlarged its premises in recent years.

An antiques and collectables market is held on Thursdays in the Long Shop. It features about fifty stalls and is a regular visiting place for London dealers. As with other similar markets such as Bermondsey and Camden Passage, it's a good idea to get here early.

Refreshment

The Commonwealth Café is a great place to go for coffee and snacks and has plenty of seating both inside and out. The massive pizza restaurant on site is very handy if you want a meal and there is also the William Morris free house towards the back of the market if you fancy a pint. The far end of the market has all kinds of food stalls serving anything from Thai curries to delicious roast pork sandwiches.

Getting a Stall

For further details about a stall at the weekend phone 020 8543 9608. If you would like a stall at the Thursday antiques and collectables market phone 07836 581 422.

southwest

135

NINE ELMS SUNDAY MARKET, SW8

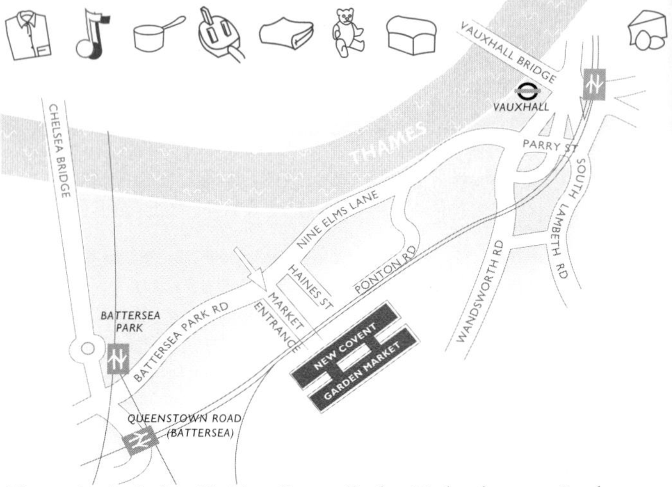

southwest

The market is sited inside New Covent Garden Market, but on a Sunday, pedestrians can't access it through the flower market complex to the north. The easiest way to get in is to follow Nine Elms Lane south for about 10 minutes, and then turn into the market's access road when you reach the Booker Cash & Carry depot on your left.

Rail: *Battersea Park*

Bus: *44, 344 (Nine Elms Lane); 77, 77a, 322 (Wandsworth Road)*

Open: *Sunday 9am-2pm*

Nine Elms market offers the sort of utility classics that street markets do best, plus a lively atmosphere and plenty of decent bric-à-brac to pick over on the car-boot stalls which share its pitch space. The problem is its location. Because it's sited in the central row of what during the week is New Covent Garden vegetable market, gaining access to Nine Elms can for pedestrians feel like trying to pick your way across a cross-channel freight depot. Once you've slogged up the access road, through the underpass, across a slip road and found a gap in the car park wall, then shimmied between a few lorry bumpers and located the right access arch – the sight of human life inside the market comes as a real relief.

And there is plenty of it: tides of people move round the large circuit of stalls in a rough-and-ready atmosphere stoked by loud music stalls and the fairground waft of fast-food vans. Nine Elms offers no real suprises as about half the stalls sell new clothes and shoes while the remainder offer standard market clobber including kitchenware, bedding, toys, fake flowers, plants, plastic bits and pieces, towels and some fairly dodgy ornaments. The clothes are incredibly cheap, with nothing much over £5. The catch is the quality. You might get the odd bargain on a pair of trainers or Birkenstock-style sandals, but there's not much to tempt anyone after something to wear from the ankles up. The ranges seem to concentrate on either mumsy dresses or barely-there teen fashions. But as with all markets, the piles of boxer shorts, ladies' underwear and socks are worth a rummage for cheap and cheerful cotton staples.

Ironically, although New Covent Garden is one of the country's largest fruit and veg wholesale markets there is only a limited range of veg on a Sunday. Still what is available is good value with a large tray of peppers for £1 and bags of bananas for the same price. Epicures will find little of appeal, but there is one stallholder selling a range of interesting-looking Mediterranean cheeses. Nine Elms also has a good selection of DIY stalls that offer serious reductions on bewildering arrays of vital tools and gismos. The CD stall has a surprisingly broad and up-to-date range of music, selling chart titles for just £10. Also have a look at the car-boot pitches to the right of the entrance. Although much of the stuff on sale is only a whisker away from being skip fodder, there are a few people offering decent retro kitchenware, clocks and small bits of furniture.

southwest

Refreshment

If you don't fancy an old-school burger or hot-dog then you could try the Market Café for a no-frills greasy brunch.

Local Attractions

Battersea Park is one of London's largest and grandest parks and is only ten minutes walk from the market.

Getting a Stall

For more details contact Bray Associates on 01895 639 912.

NORTHCOTE ROAD, SW11

North end of Northcote Road

Rail: *Clapham Junction (Victoria, Waterloo)*
Bus: *35, 156, 170, 219, 295, C3 (Clapham Junction);*
49, 239, 319, 337, G1 (Northcote Road)
Open: *Monday-Saturday 9am-5pm, Wednesday 9am-1pm*

Northcote Road has undergone something of a revolution in the last decade with what was once an ordinary market street now a bustling strip of slick shops and eateries which are very much a focus for SW11's smart set. The transformation of the area with the arrival of smart deli's and gift shops on a tidal wave of cappuccino froth was initially a bad thing for the old street market, but in recent years the market has staged something of a revival with trade being restricted very largely to a Friday and Saturday, with only a few fruit and veg stalls from Thursday to Saturday and the large flower stall being the only trader to do business seven days a week. It's regrettable that the old weekday market has largely disappeared, but the concentration of activity to a Friday and Saturday and a change in the nature of the stalls has given the street market a new lease of life.

southwest

The fruit and veg traders around Mallinson Road form the heart of the market and are the longest serving pitches, trading from ancient wooden carved stalls which have been in the same family for several generations. The traders of the past would probably be a bit baffled by the artichokes, asparagus, celeriac and oyster mushrooms which are now evident on the stalls and popular among the smart crowd which shop here on a weekend. The fruit and veg dealers are now kept company by a range of stalls catering for the new denizens of SW11 with a photographer displaying a vast selection of his black and white photographs, framed examples of which can be bought for £35. Another trader specialises in hand-painted, colourful crockery while the stall next to his offered jars of prepared French food like paté and ratatouille at prices which reflected the high quality of the produce.

Proceeding further north there are more stalls that exemplify the change the market has undergone in recent years. A fantastic toy dealer offers a selection of handmade wooden toys with small cars for £8 and going up to several hundred pounds for a large wooden representation of Noah and his Ark, complete with menagerie. The jewellery stall is also rather smart with stock from a number of independent jewellery makers and rings starting from a very reasonable £15 and necklaces from £25. On the corner of Shelgate Road is a large display of bread and pastry, but again the slant is towards a moneyed clientele with chiabatta and almond croissant to the fore. It's easy to dismiss these stalls as catering for yuppies, but it's difficult to complain about the disappearing working-class culture with a mouth full of fresh croissant.

Further along is a more basic fruit and veg stall which is kept company by a fancy deli stall offering olives, salads, feta cheese and other delicacies all displayed in large wooden vats. One of the best stalls on the street and one typical of the change in the market is the one selling fashionable clothes, raffia bags, scarves and Chinese flip-flops and trading under the name Bag Lady. The goods are great quality and it's encouraging to see someone re-thinking how to sell goods from a street market with the stall painted an eyecatching bright red and the wares well displayed. After Cairns Road stands the massive flower stall, which is the only stall on the market still trading seven days a week. The range of cut

southwest

flowers and potted plants is huge and the father and son team that run the stall proffer plenty of advice and can prepare bouquets to order. The market finishes with a new arrival called Funky Mama and true to its name offers a range of funky woman's T-Shirts, skirts and also a limited range of baby shoes. The young woman running the stall has ambitious plans to decorate it and reports that the nearby shops have been very helpful and welcoming, which is a refreshing change from the rancour that usually exists between shops and stalls at more traditional markets.

Northcote Road Market is a market on the up and it seems a pity that the council are restricting many of the traders to Friday and Saturday. After visiting so many markets and encountering so much despondency (some of it justified) from stall-holders, it is joy to experience a market with a more positive atmosphere. It would probably benefit some market traders to visit Northcote Road on a Saturday, just to see how some stalls are adapting to modern times.

Refreshment
There are so many trendy cafés on Northcote Road that the one thing you will have no problem getting is refreshment. Among the best places to eat is the smart café selling slices of pizza and coffee and calling itself Slice. Another very popular place to eat is the Gourmet Burger Kitchen which does fancy burgers at an equally fancy price.

Local Attractions
There are some fantastic food shops along Northcote Road which complement the market. Among the best of these is Hamish Johnston, the very fine deli on the corner of Shelgate Road and the traditional butchers at the top of the market. If you like rummaging for second-hand things, there are several good charity shops on the street which, being located in such a posh area, tend to stock a better class of cast-off.

Getting a Stall
For further details contact Wandsworth Council (see appendix).

WIMBLEDON STADIUM

Wimbledon Stadium car park, Plough Lane
Rail: Haydons Road
Bus: 44, 77, 155, 270, 280, G1
Open: Sunday 9am-2pm

If you have an image of Wimbledon which involves manicured lawns, ivy covered buildings and strawberries and cream, then Wimbledon Stadium Sunday market is going to be a shock. The stadium is a modern and fairly uninteresting building and it is surrounded by an equally unimpressive urban landscape. About 150 stalls set up in the concrete car park alongside the stadium every Sunday, offering a wide selection of new goods and food. The only thing this market has in common with the hallowed ground of SW19, is that it also sells strawberries – although at £1.50 a large box, rather than a fiver for a small bowl.

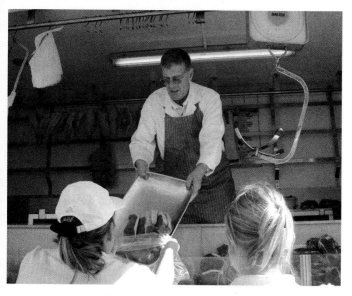

As you enter the market your attention will be drawn to the large lorry selling cheap electronic goods. The diminutive salesman is a real pro and always has a large crowd of eager punters hanging on his every word. "Ladies and gents, take a look at this. A Goodmans set top box which allows you access to all the top channels and once you've got the box you don't pay a thing – not one thing, totally free. This box sells for £120 on the High Street and that is not one word of a lie. I could sell you this box for half-price – just £60. Wait sir, wait, I haven't finished, put your money away! I'm not going to do that. No sir. I'm not going to sell it for £55, not £50, not £45...no, no, no. That's right madam, here today it's just £40, that right just £40. That's right, one at a time please..." With that five people had raised their hands in the air and he had just taken £200 in two minutes. I can't vouch for the apparent bargains he offers, but it's great entertainment to watch him sell.

Other things to be found at this market include cheap street fashion, all kinds of shoe, a more limited range of plants and garden ornaments, brightly coloured nylon rugs, leather jackets and bags, vacuum cleaner accessories, small electrical goods for the kitchen, videos, household goods and bedding. The shoe stalls were particularly impressive with several really large displays and plenty of good deals for around a tenner. The trader selling household electrics avoided any sales spiel, but had some attractive deals like a DeLonghi coffee maker for only £24.99 and a Phillips iron for £14. There are numerous stalls flogging cheap street fashion, but much of it is dull and synthetic. Look out for pitches selling designer label copies, many of which are good quality and include things like faux Nike T-shirts for only a tenner.

Wimbledon Stadium mainly deals in consumer durables, but there are enough good food stalls to make this a market worth visiting for essentials. Carnivores are particularly well catered for with several established butchers' lorries offering deals like two legs of lamb for only £12 and ten beef steaks for just a tenner. There are only two fruit and veg stalls on the market but both are huge and feature some great bargains including big bags of potatoes for £6.50, 2lb of plums for £1.20 and 3lb of onions for just 50p. The only exotic comestibles were found at the olive and feta cheese stall and the pitch given over to dried fruits and nuts. Both stalls were quiet with the average punter here preferring basics to anything fancy. Most passers-by turned their noses up even when offered a free taster.

Refreshment

The pervasive smell of burgers and sausages is an indication of the type of food on offer here, but there are a few alternatives such as the Thai food stall and the burger stall which also offers salt beef.

Getting a Stall

For further details contact Sherman Waterman Associates Ltd who can be reached on 020 7240 7405.

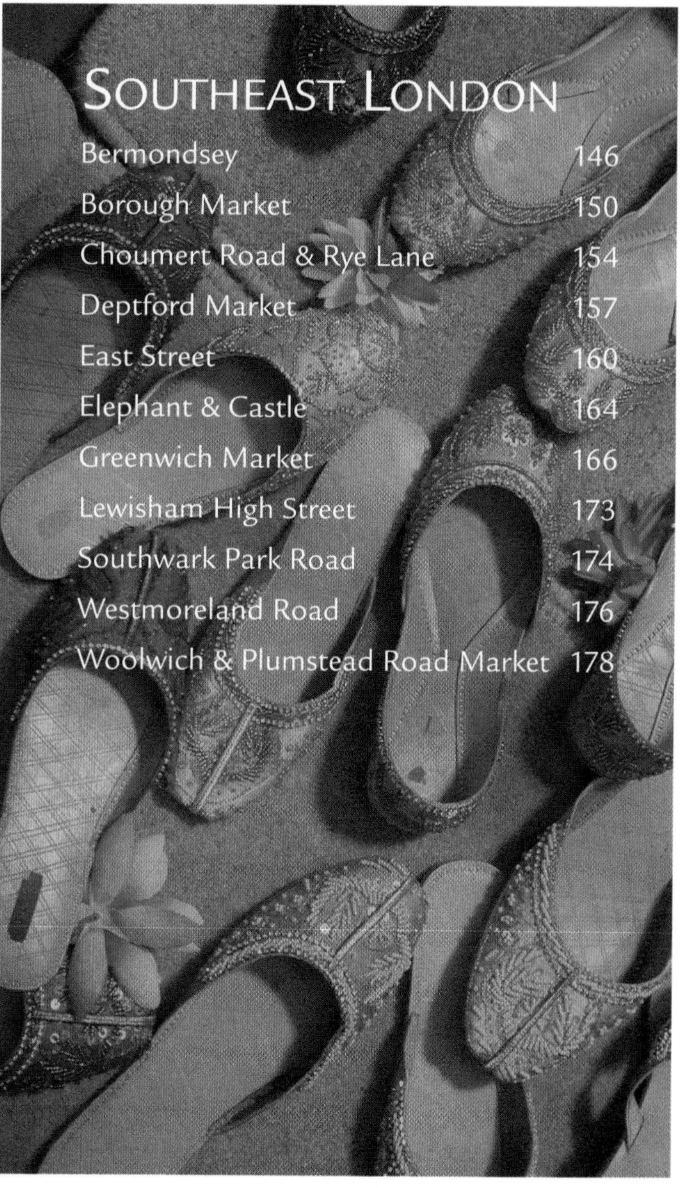

SOUTHEAST LONDON

Bermondsey 146

Borough Market 150

Choumert Road & Rye Lane 154

Deptford Market 157

East Street 160

Elephant & Castle 164

Greenwich Market 166

Lewisham High Street 173

Southwark Park Road 174

Westmoreland Road 176

Woolwich & Plumstead Road Market 178

southeast

BERMONDSEY, SE1

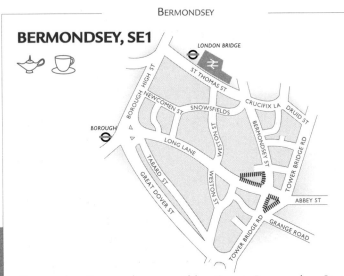

Bermondsey Square, between Abbey Street, Bermondsey Street and Tower Bridge Street

Tube: Borough, London Bridge (Northern)

Rail: London Bridge

Bus: 1, 42, 188 (Tower Bridge Street); 1, 78 (Grange Road)

Open: Fridays 5am-1pm

The whiff of a dodgy reputation still lingers around the capital's largest (and cheapest) antiques market at Bermondsey Square – maybe it's the location, tucked south of the river in deepest SE1, or the fact that in winter the market kicks off in pre-dawn darkness, with dealers setting up from as early as 3.30am. Visitors hoping for a glimpse of illicit London will be disappointed, as Bermondsey Market is in fact the centre of a very serious antiques trade; the atmosphere in this attractive square is far more like a civilised continental flea market than a wideboys' dealing den. That said, a lot of money changes hands as large numbers of focused buyers regularly come from abroad to pick up cheap items from the mass of antiques on show: displays encompass an almost overwhelming range of silver, jewellery, clocks, glass, prints, crockery and porcelain. A lot of well-informed scrutinising goes on down every row of stalls, as people pick over thousands of collectables.

Although a lot of business takes place before dawn, the market continues to trade until lunch time and on a recent visit actually became more crowded after 9 o'clock. It is during the daylight hours that a more relaxed crowd flocks to the market to stroll among the stalls. Many of the visitors are tourists and it is worth the effort of visiting the market to witness a stall-holder negotiating a price with a Japanese visitor without the aid of a common language and instead reverting to a kind of primitive sign language. At another stall a trader took a very much more direct approach with a curious punter, "that's fifty pounds" and when she started walking away, "do you like it, and do you have cash?" When she replied in the affirmative he closed in for the kill and managed to get £42 for a large 1930's vase. The antiques trade has a rather cut-throat reputation, but there seems to be a good deal of cama-raderie at the market with traders asking each others advice about the value of a particular item and even discussing how much money they have taken.

Prices reflect the quality of the goods, with few glaring bargains jumping out from the spread of beautiful and unusual pieces. Although friendly, it's unlikely dealers will do you many favours, especially on more unique objects, but appealing items can still be picked up for under a tenner. Bargains on a recent visit included an attractive contem-porary oil painting for £75, sets of silver cutlery for £7 and even some modern electronic goods with one stall offering a selection of Roberts radios for £10 each. Shopping around can also reduce prices signifi-cantly, so don't go for the first example of something you like – it may well be £5 cheaper on a nearby stall. The costume jewellery is particu-larly interesting, with a lot of out of the ordinary pieces, for example, twenties vulcanite (a coal-based plastic) chain-link necklaces were going for around £35. It's refreshing that despite being a market full of antiques, outcrops of genuine idiosyncrasy are everywhere at Bermondsey, with old German microscopes sitting alongside collectable Dinky Toys, and a Barbie doll with her plastic chest exposed to the elements, next to a fine set of chess pieces.

Refreshment

Food provision in the immediate area of the market is pretty functional, but you can get a solid breakfast for well under a fiver at the trader's favourite, Rose Dining Room on Bermondsey Street, or in the Indoor Market's coffee shop (on Long Lane). If you don't mind eating alfresco the catering van that is situated in the centre of the market does a good cuppa and bacon sandwich. Further away, Manze on the south end of Tower Bridge Street offers an authentic pie and mash experience for around £2, but doesn't open till 10am which is a little late for early visitors to the market. Delfina Trust Studios is at the north end of Bermondsey Street and houses a contemporary art gallery as well as a restaurant that serves great coffee.

Local Attractions

The antiques trade also bleeds out into the streets around Bermondsey Square with large, warren-like warehouses on Long Lane, Bermondsey Street and the north section of Tower Bridge Street chaotically full of furniture and larger pieces of household kit. Prices won't impress the seasoned junk-buyer and the emphasis seems to be on fairly heavy, dark wood pieces but, if you persevere, you can probably find something interesting and of good quality for a reasonable price. If after a few hours pottering you can bear yet more antiques, The Indoor Market on Long Lane has some quirky specialisms, with the clothes unit next to the entrance (nearest the corner of Long Lane and Bermondsey Street) stocking theatrically glamorous retro clothes and fabrics.

Getting a Stall

For further details contact Southwark Council (see appendix).

southeast

BOROUGH MARKET, SE1

Southwark Street, SE1
Tube: London Bridge (Northern and Jubilee)
Rail: London Bridge
Bus: 21, 35, 40, 47, 133, 343, 381
Open: Friday noon-6pm, Saturday 9am-4pm

At the heart of Southwark and across the street from London Bridge Station, Borough Market has been trading in this spot since 1756 and is the oldest established fruit and vegetable wholesale market in central London. Today what was once a place for traders from all over England and the globe to trade cattle, grain and fish has become a foodie mecca for professional chefs and weekend gourmets. Monmouth Coffee, Neal's Yard Dairy, Konditor & Cook and other luxury food shops line the edges of the market. Part weekday wholesale market, part weekend gourmet food market, Borough caters to a large population.

150

Of interest to most is the Friday and Saturday market, which is open to the public. The wholesale market is open to retailers and restaurateurs in the early hours of the morning. On Friday and Saturday, the market gets packed with people so it's best to come as early as possible. However, the late afternoon bustle does lend an electric atmosphere to the place.

The choice of products is vast and rather sophisticated. While it's possible to do your weekly shopping here, it's best to visit for speciality ingredients and exotic treats. Foreign cuisines from all over the globe are represented: German, Greek, Indian, Italian, Middle-Eastern, Spanish, Malaysian, South-East Asian, Swedish and West Indian. There's even a supplier of honey made from London bees.

For beverages, try French wines before you buy or pick up some imported beer with unusual flavours like honey or raspberry. The Monmouth Coffee shop flanks the market, but there's an aromatic stall in the market as well. Knowledgeable coffee drinkers staff the coffee booth and are happy to help you choose the best bean. For a refreshing and healthy smoothie, try the Natural Juice Bar trolley.

southeast

At the half dozen or so fish stalls, razor-toothed monkfish sit flanked by local crab and giant Saudi prawns. Cooked scallops and dressed crab are particularly good choices for fresh cooked snacks. However, the star attraction of the snacks is the grilled chorizo sandwich with rocket and divine olive oil from Brindisa, stockists of a variety of Spanish products. At places like the Ginger Pig stall, game like venison and ostrich (even the eggs are for sale) and lamb feature heavily as do a variety of homemade sausages with flavours like pork and apple.

Excellent baked goods from rich chocolate cakes to simple pain au levain are much in evidence – temptation for even the strongest of wills. Seriously decadent truffles and chocolates vie for attention along with pre-made puddings ready to heat up at home. Gourmands in search of unusual and speciality cheese won't be dissapointed either with a plethora of cheeses sourced from all over Britain and Europe.

Fruit and veg are brilliant as well. The tomatoes from the Isle of Wight have an unbeatable depth of flavour while the olive stalls sell fabulous stuffed olives. Tiny wild strawberries, baby aubergines and wild asparagus sit alongside tried-and-true English produce like apples from Chegworth Valley and luscious cabbages, carrots and beets. Mushroom lovers will delight in the huge selection of fresh chanterelles, pied bleu, porcini and more.

Perhaps one of the most exotic stalls is the Cool Chile Co. that sells products from Mexico and Central America. Occasionally, they have fresh tomatillos, but they are always well-stocked with dried chillies of every description as well as prepared spice mixes and rich cornmeal tortillas. Another virtually unheard of ingredient available here is argan oil handpressed from the nuts of the argan tree in North Africa. The smooth, nutty flavour is perfect for dipping or for topping squash soup. Even humble muesli is sold at one stall devoted to a variety of the cereal's incarnations.

Getting a Stall

Contact Borough Market on Tel. 020 747 1002 to enquire about renting a stall at either the wholesale or gourmet markets.

southeast

CHOUMERT ROAD, SE15

a) Choumert Rd
b) Rye Lane

Rye Lane end of Choumert Road, and Atwell Road opposite
Rail: *Peckham Rye (London Bridge)*
Bus: *12, 37, 63, 78, 312, 343, P12 (Rye Lane)*
Open: *Monday-Saturday 9.30am-5pm*

One of London's Chartered Markets, Choumert Road has been the site of a provisions market for well over a hundred years. Many of the fifteen or so stalls that set up here are old, wooden carts which have been wheeled around the market for so many years that the wooden wheels are almost worn to the axle. The old stalls have seen a lot of changes in the market as well as in the make-up of the local community. The resulting influx of international food shops into the area has meant that goods at Choumert Road are now just one of many options amidst a bewildering tide of multi-cultural foodstuffs engulfing both Rye Lane and the roads which run off it. But despite massive competition the market looks as though it has enough scruffy charisma to keep it alive at least until the wheels finally fall off the wagon.

The stalls (pitched close to the row of specialist food shops to create a colourful corridor of produce) still attract a steady flow of customers with plenty of bargains and friendly banter. Times have changed so a lot more than just the humble spud or greens are on offer in the market. Put together the range available is like a United Nations of fruit and veg: whether you're cooking Moroccan, Thai or Afro-Caribbean, one of Choumert Road's traders should be able to supply the ingredients.

Even if you're not buying, just walking through the stalls is a real foodie treat, with loads of unusual shapes and smells to savour. Local rivalry keeps the prices pretty cheap, five large juicy sweetcorn sell for £1 and a massive watermelon for £2.90. Across Rye Lane at the end of Atwell Street there is an additional fruit and veg stall which has the locals queuing up, so shop around.

There were once several stalls selling consumer durables, but these were not in evidence on a recent visit, although I was assured that they do occasionally make an appearance.

Refreshment
There are several rather down-at-heel eating places on Choumert Road, but none of them seemed very inviting. Those looking to eat and drink in a pleasant environment should walk 5 minutes along Choumert Road onto Bellenden Road which has several smart cafés.

Local Attractions
There is a good butchers on Choumert Road offering poultry and other staples as well as more exotic things like pigs' feet and cows' tongues. D.G. Wheeler is a long established fishmonger which has adapted to the needs of the local population stocking jack fish and red mullet alongside cod and haddock.

Getting a Stall
For further details contact Southwark Council (see Appendix)

southeast

RYE LANE, SE15

48 Rye Lane, between
Elm Grove and High Shore Road
Rail: Peckham Rye
Bus: 12, 37, 63, 78, 312, 343, P12
Open: Monday-Saturday 9am-6pm

In 2000 the market shut for a major refurbishment. The new market is a much more attractive place to shop. The entrance has kept the same Art Deco design but in place of peeling plaster and a tatty sign, is a clean white exterior with a stylish steel arch. Inside the market the improvement is even more evident with a glass roofed passageway leading to a main hall with about 50 clean, new units. The central part of this L shaped market is still a little dark, but the painted floors and bright lighting have banished the grim and rather damp atmosphere of the old market.

It would be good if the stall-holders within the market had sharpened up their act to match the new environment, but the traders have not changed much and the new building is quiet even on a Friday afternoon when Rye Lane is busy. Among the things on offer are mobile phone accessories, a selection of household goods and toiletries, carpets, pet food and accessories, a black music stall, shoes, street fashion and African food-stuffs. The unit selling stylish Italian-made, men's shoes for only £25 a pair, stood out as the best value. Sadly, the tool outlet and the one selling small electronic goods were both very poorly stocked and the traders seemed suspicious that anyone should be showing an interest in their goods. The main problem with this market is that there are none of the market staples that would encourage regular visits.

Refreshment

Le Petit Jardin Café is a pleasant if inappropriately named café in the middle of the market which serves a good cappuccino.

Getting a Stall

For further details contact the market office on 020 7732 2202.

DEPTFORD MARKET, SE8

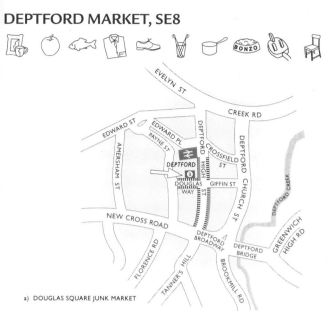

a) DOUGLAS SQUARE JUNK MARKET

Deptford High Street (Deptford Broadway to Deptford Station)

Rail: *Deptford*

Bus: *47, 53, 177, 188, 199, 225*

Open: *Wednesday, Friday and Saturday 8.30am-5pm*

Although Deptford is just a fifteen minute bus ride from Greenwich, it has none of its famous neighbour's tourist attractions and its market is largely unknown outside the area. The market itself is huge, extending over half the length of Deptford High Street and also along Douglas Way – including a large flea market in Douglas Square on Wednesdays and Saturdays. The combination of a lively street market offering good quality standard market fare, along with a cheap and dirty junk market is a good one. A visitor to Deptford on a Saturday can do all the weekly essential shopping, but also indulge in the hunt for inexpensive bric-à-brac. Markets that offer this kind of interesting shopping are rare these days and Deptford is beginning to stand out as one of the best such markets to visit on a Saturday.

Deptford Church Street and Douglas Way

The main thoroughfares of the market have over 150 stalls offering a great selection of basics like fresh fruit and veg, fresh fish, street fashion, bags and shoes, toiletries and household goods, perfume, watches, pet food and accessories. The market also has some outstanding specialist stalls dealing in car accessories, household blinds and including a very well-stocked stall offering cheap, boxed vacuum cleaners and accessories as well as small kitchen electricals with a brand name toaster for only £12. The top end of the market even had a trader selling beds, with a choice of four styles standing on the pavement. Although many markets have stalls selling pots and pans, Deptford had on offer just about the largest cooking pot known to man for a mere £60. Cooking pans large enough to feed an army are not going to be of general interest, but it is an indication of the range of wares to be found at the market. Some of the best value clothing stalls are on Douglas Way with one stall offering a good selection of skirts and dresses for just £5 each and another trader stocking good quality Nike T-shirts for only a tenner. The best buy went to the stall selling a well made Kickers pull-over jacket for only £7.99.

Douglas Square Flea Market

Every Wednesday and Saturday Douglas Square is filled with about 40 stalls offering a sprawling assortment of bric-à-brac, used clothing, electrical goods, videos, jewellery and furniture. No attempt to display the goods is really made with clothes piled high on tables, and boxes of assorted items just put on the floor. The huge library bookshelf on wheels for only £30 was a great buy – similar items sell for around £100 in retro furniture stores. A sturdy old Singer sewing machine in working order was only a fiver, and a large unmarked fish tank could be picked-up here for the same price. The smaller bric-à-brac was all at jumble sale prices with just about any item of clothing for £1, assorted table glasses for 50p and a mixed selection of golf clubs for just 50p each. The flea market starts and finishes earlier than the rest of Deptford Market, even on fine summer days traders start packing up by 2.30 in the afternoon.

Refreshment

Hales Gallery keeps the art in the basement, reserving the ground floor for a spacious café with a garden at the back. The Deptford Arms is just a few doors down and serves a good pint. If you don't mind eating on the go, the Thai food stall on Douglas Way is clean and popular.

Local Attractions

There are lots of decent food shops along Deptford High Street that add to the market's appeal, including several good butchers, fishmongers and one specialising in farm fresh eggs. If the flea market hasn't exhausted your thirst for second-hand goods there are several excellent charity shops along the High Street. Those interested in modern art should take the opportunity to visit Hales Gallery at 70 Deptford High Street.

Getting a Stall

For further details contact Lewisham Council (see Appendix)

EAST STREET, SE17

East Street between Walworth Road and Dawes Street
Tube: Elephant & Castle (Northern, Bakerloo)
Bus: 12, 35, 40, 45, 68, 171, 176, 468, X68 (Walworth Road);
42, 343 (Thurlow Road)
Open: Tuesday-Sunday 8.30am-4pm (busiest at weekends, when the street's shops are open both days)

The birthplace of Charlie Chaplin, East Street is also home to one of South London's biggest, busiest and loudest markets. At weekends, with stalls squeezed between shops along the length of this long street, it begins to look like Oxford Street in miniature – tides of determined shoppers weave around clumps of slow-moving bargain hunters as the queues build for cut-price essentials. Surrounded by some of the area's largest housing estates, East Street has a long history of serving the practical needs of local people, so craft fair trinkets are nowhere to be seen on stalls crammed with all things useful, wearable or edible.

southeast

Unlike a lot of other markets, in East Street you can still find a genuine sense of community, with lots of classic South London humour, a real mix of shoppers, plenty of banter and noisily competitive traders stoking the lively atmosphere. The market isn't a wise choice for the delicate or the hung over, as one lady sighed recently as she entered the Saturday scrum at the Walworth Road junction: "...this place is no good for my nerves." On busy days you will need to watch out for serious jostlers, and East Street can also bring new meaning to the phrase "price wars" as you get caught in the crossfire between sellers as "Oi! Come on, who wants a bargain?", "Two pounds of mush' a nicker" punch repeatedly into the air above your head. But the demonstrations of iron-larynxed stamina and word-mangling delivery make brilliant free entertainment. My favourite is the burly fruit and veg man at the far end of the market who makes good comic use of his incongruously high-pitched voice to draw in the punters.

The size of the market means that rival traders have to compete on price, so make sure you don't part with your cash without first checking out the opposition. The market is surprisingly long and from its start on Walworth Road it's quite a trek to the far end, at the junction with Dawes Street. East Street offers all the staples characteristic of any large street market, with lots of great bargains for the discerning shopper amongst piles of household and electrical goods, CDs, bedding and carpets, sweets, luggage, perfume, toiletries, jewellery, toys, fruit and veg (some Caribbean as well as standard English), wholesale meat, plants and flowers. The local Chinese community are also beginning to make their presence felt on the market with some very fine Oriental handbags for only £7 and another stall offering Chinese medicine with things like tea that claims to help discourage smoking.

Certain things do stand out. East Street is full of clothes, and many of the shops and stalls offer impressive reductions on chain store prices – underwear, dresses, and shirts are often good value – although sifting is essential as much of the stock is definitely more cheap than chic. A number of haberdashery and material stalls – as well as the excellent Barney's Textile Centre – also offer D.I.Y. fashion bunnies the chance to create some pretty snazzy outfits. One of the longest running haberdashers is run by an elderly and almost deaf trader who makes a great display of his wares from his ancient wooden stall and offers most items for between 50p and £1. The shoe stalls also carry an impressive range with some persuasive prices like smart women's dress shoes for £12 and other more basic footwear for only £5 a pair. Sundays also provide the chance to kit out your garden or window box on the cheap, as a high tide of very reasonably priced plants washes into Blackwood Street, half-way along the market – pick up trays of Busy Lizzies or daisy bushes for under a fiver.

Refreshment

Once you've battled through the bargains, East Street isn't short of culinary pit stops. Right along its length, the market is dotted with pubs, stalls and cafés. Local favourites include the Market Grill, Maries Snack Bar and the Golden Café all of which offer good basic grub. For food on the go there is the long established East Street Burger Stand which is towards the far end of the market.

Local Attractions

The is not much to attract visitors to this part of town, but on a Sunday Westmoreland Road Market is well worth a visit if you like sifting through junk for bargains (see page 176).

Getting a Stall

For further details contact Southwark Council (see appendix).

ELEPHANT & CASTLE, SE1

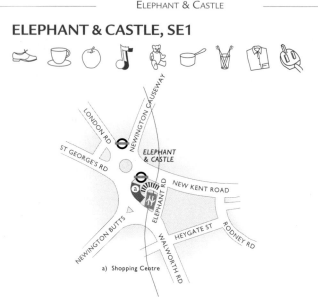

a) Shopping Centre

Outside Elephant & Castle shopping centre

Tube: Elephant & Castle (Northern and Bakerloo)
Rail: Elephant & Castle (Blackfriars)
Bus: 1, 12, 35, 45, 53, 63, 68, 100, 155, 168, 171, 172, 176, 188, 322, 344, C10, X68
Open: Monday-Saturday 9.30am-5pm

This market, which circles at below ground level outside the famous shopping centre at Elephant and Castle, is a fairly recent arrival to the area. Unfortunately, its location – stuck under the centre's concrete petticoats with the smell of the municipal toilet never far away – hasn't helped to establish much of an atmosphere. People surfacing out of the labyrinthine tunnels under the Elephant's twin roundabouts seem mainly concentrated on getting either to or from work or in or out of Tesco Metro, so you don't feel very encouraged to potter. The selection of goods on offer is pretty uninspiring, focusing on new clothes, sportswear, accessories, jewellery, watches, toys, electrical and household goods and toiletries – you might uncover the odd genuine bargain if you persevere. One such find were the Kangol T-shirts recently spotted here for only £3 each.

On the sartorial front, some stalls stock slightly more interesting and fashionable women's clothes, but the emphasis is on cheap, functional separates aimed generally at a more middle-aged customer. A few traders have £1 rails or jumble-style trestles with mixes of second-hand clothes, but there are few choice items in amongst the nylon nasties of yesteryear. The large shoe stall had some reasonable deals, but there was nothing exceptional among its stock. If you find the hectic atmosphere of the market a little too much, one of the stalls offered massages, with a 6 minute massage for £6.

southeast

Refreshment

As well as the Latin food outlets in the shopping centre the market also has a good selection of lively food stalls, selling either Thai, Caribbean or African snacks.

Local Attractions

Although the market isn't worth a special visit, if you do happen to pass through and have time to kill, take a quick look in the shopping centre itself. It may be a much-maligned example of soulless retail architecture, but the Elephant's infamous centrepiece hides a few things that counter the general tone of strip-lit blandness. Opposite Woolworth's, Tlon Books stocks a surprisingly comprehensive selection of competitively priced second-hand fiction and non-fiction titles, catering well for people on the look out for the idiosyncratic as well as the classic. The first floor of the centre has become a meeting place for Peckham's Latin American community with a great Latin Music outlet and several places to get authentic Latin food and coffee.

Getting a Stall

For further details about getting a stall phone 020 7708 2313.

GREENWICH MARKET, SE10

a) Royal Charter Market
b) Central Market
c) Antique Market

Greenwich Church Street, Stockwell Street, Greenwich High Road

Rail: Greenwich (London Bridge), Island Gardens (Docklands Light Railway and take foot tunnel to Greenwich)

Bus: 177, 180, 188, 199, 286, 386

River Boat: This is a great way to see the Thames and visit the market. There are riverboats running from Westminster, Embankment and Tower pier every Sunday to Greenwich. For details contact Greenwich Tourist Office on 020 8858 6376

Open: Saturday and Sunday 9.30am-5pm (all parts of the market)
Thursday 9.30am-5pm (collectables market within the Charter Market)
Friday 9am-5pm (crafts market within the Charter Market)

G reenwich has a fantastic market and in recent years it seems to have improved after a slight dip in fortunes in the late 90's. Like other major markets Greenwich is not so much one market as several offering different things and open at varying times. It is only on a Sunday that all parts of the market are in full swing. Greenwich is often compared to Camden and Portobello, but it is unique, not least because of its maritime history and its location on the Thames offering spectacular views of the City (best enjoyed from the top of Greenwich Park). The Thames is ever present here and gives the place a seaside atmosphere – particularly on fine days when it is like a cross between Portobello Market and Brighton seafront. If you visit on a Thursday or Friday only the Charter Market will be open, and Greenwich will seem rather quiet and restful. On Saturdays the Charter Market is joined by the Central and Antique Markets although both markets are not fully occupied with stalls and there is still room for a leisurely wander. On Sundays Greenwich is at its busiest If you don't like crowds and the hustle and bustle of a busy market, Saturday might be the best day to visit, but for those that want to get the whole Greenwich experience, Sunday is the day to go. Below are reviews for all parts of the market with their opening times.

The Royal Charter Market (formerly the Crafts Market)

Entrances on Greenwich Church Street, College Approach, King William Walk and Nelson Road

Open: Thursday 7.30am-5pm (antiques and collectables),
Friday-Sunday 9.30-5pm (arts and crafts)

The name of this market derives from the royal charter of 1700 that sanctioned a market to be held here – although in those days it traded wholesale in fruit and veg rather than the arts, crafts and collectables of today. The buildings around the courtyard have not changed and the cobbled stones and paving are still original, but a modern roof has been added in the last 20 years which lets in natural light while keeping out the elements.

The arts and crafts market occupies the courtyard at weekends and carries a great selection of original things among its 50 or 60 stalls. Barbara Stewart's stall offered handmade hats for as little as £10 with more elaborate examples going for £25. The leather stall was not selling its own work but still represented great value with leather jackets from around £59 and modern leather bags for £20. Another stall was selling their own simple women's dresses made from Irish linen for only £30, which was a snip considering the quality. If you've got kids in tow there are plenty of things here to interest them with lots of toys and clothing available, my favourite being the Chinese kite stall offering beautiful silk kites with traditional designs for just £6.50. There was also a stall selling brightly coloured plastic bathroom sundries like brushes and toothmugs for under a fiver, which would appeal to most kids and might even encourage them to brush their hair. One of the best value stalls had simple wooden bowls and containers at very keen prices, including a large fruit bowl made from dark mango wood for only £15. The market can boast a great many unusual things not to be found at any other market, and this included the stall trading in colourful butterflies and other insects mounted on card and framed for as little as £10. Framed insects aren't everyone's cup of tea, but if they appeal to you, the Charter Market is just about the only place in town to find such things.

One of the welcome changes to the market in recent years has been the addition of a selection of food stalls at the College Approach entrance to the market. It is here you can find fresh bread and pastries, handmade biscuits, fine cheeses and cured meats, Turkish pastries, flavoured oils and chutneys, Russian delicacies and a stall specialising in sausages including a variety of veggie bangers. The food is of excellent quality and it's great to find a market offering extravagant gifts as well as practical things like food.

The antiques and collectables market held here on a Thursday is ideal if you want to avoid the Sunday crowds. About forty stalls set up here selling all kinds of things such as cheap paperbacks, classical CDs from £4, interesting old toys and collectables from seventies kitsch articles to Russian oil paintings from the thirties. Compared to weekends, on a Thursday the market is very quiet with stall-holders reading the papers or chatting with an occasional customer and plenty of tables available at The Meeting House Café.

Refreshment

One of the best things about this market is its relaxed atmosphere and numerous eating and drinking venues. Among the places to sit and relax with a pint and your purchases are The Coach and Horses and Admiral Hardy pubs, or try the Meeting House Café housed within the market. Just outside the market on Nelson Road and on the way to the Central Market is Café Pistachios which is an established favourite and has a large garden dining area.

Getting a Stall

For further details contact the market office on 020 8293 3110, or try the company's head office on 020 7515 7153.

southeast

The Central Market
Stockwell Street

Open: Saturday-Sunday 9am-5pm

The Central Market is the largest part of Greenwich market and offers an eclectic mix of furniture, new and second-hand clothing, bric-à-brac, collectable vinyl, CDs and books. The main entrance is on Stockwell Street and is identified by the Village Market building which was once a fine book market but which in recent years has been given over to Indonesian furniture. If this isn't your thing it is probably better that you move a little further on to the courtyard where stands the South London Book Centre which offers a fantastic selection of used books at reasonable prices. It has been joined in recent years by a great retro shop called Twinkled which sells all kinds of 50's-80's furniture and homewares over two floors and often spreads out onto the pavement outside with some of the larger furniture. Another welcome addition to the market has been the fruit and veg stall which offers a good selection of all your favourite edible flora.

Walking further into the market you will encounter lots of stalls offering bric-à-brac, vinyl and smaller pieces of furniture. Interesting things found here recently included an old, cast-iron stove for £110 and a large dark wood ornamental bull for only £10. Look out for a huge plastic model of a Japanese geisha girl complete with revolving head – it is one of the landmarks of the market and stands just outside an indoor furniture centre which offers a mix of new reproduction furniture along with a few genuine antiques.

The large open square at the back is the heart of the Central Market and is occupied with stalls offering bric-à-brac, retro clothing and furniture. This is a great place to look for quirky bargains with odd things being sold from boxes on the pavement for just a few quid and plenty of discount rails flogging clothes for just £1. From here the market spreads out in two directions. The other side of the Village Market building is more dedicated to youth culture with endless stalls selling new fashion, sunglasses and CDs, as well as one or two retro clothing stalls. The stall selling retro men's clothing is well worth having a look at with a great selection of shirts for £12-£15. In the other direction in the far corner of the market stands the entrance to an indoor complex with stalls offering collectables, new clothing, second-hand furniture and contemporary gifts with a slightly hippy flavour – things like strange smoking devices and joss sticks. This part of the market leads through to King William Walk which in turn leads to the wonderful Greenwich Park if you fancy a break from shopping. If you still have an appetite for more marketeering cut back to Greenwich High Street, where you will find the Antiques Market.

southeast

Refreshment

The Central Market has a number of good food stalls, the most estab-lished being the Thai stall at the back of the market. There is also a collection of food stalls just on the corner of Stockwell Road offering all kinds international food. Just opposite is Café Rouge which serves fancy French grub at a fairly high price. There is also Café Pistachios on Nelson Road which is a firm favourite.

Getting a Stall

To get a stall at the Central Market just turn up by 8.30am and ask to speak to the market manager.

Greenwich Antiques Market
Greenwich High Road (next to the cinema)
Open: Saturday and Sunday 9am-5pm

This part of the market offers a far wider selection of goods than its name suggests. On a busy Sunday about fifty stalls set up here, although there are fewer on a Saturday and being open air this part of the market is vulnerable to the weather. On a good day you can find retro clothes, very fine new and antique bed linen, antique cutlery, some interesting pieces of furniture, books, a stall specialising in framed mirrors, and several dealers in old postcards, coins and other collectables. The stall offering a selection of old hand tools would appeal to DIY buffs with lots of well maintained wooden handled chisels for £10 each. One of the best aspects of this market is the selection of collectable and costume jewellery at reasonable prices, including a fine vintage amber bracelet for only £24. There is one trader who sells oil paintings from his stall at the market with all the charm and gentility of an art gallery and stocks anything from a small watercolour for £5 to a large contemporary oil painting for £800. The CD and tape stall showed equal discrimination in its selection of stock with an emphasis on Jazz, Gospel and Classical music. This is one of the best parts of Greenwich market, but is a little off the main path followed by visitors and for this reason traders are often willing to barter and there are always one or two stalls selling items to clear.

Refreshment
Next door to the market is The Market public house which also has seating outside for fine weather.

Local Attractions
There is much for the visitor to enjoy in Greenwich besides the market, including the National Maritime Museum, Fan Museum, Cutty Sark and The Royal Observatory. For more details about exploring Greenwich contact the Greenwich Tourist Office (020 8858 6376).

Getting a Stall
For further details about Greenwich Antiques Market contact Jane on 020 7237 2001.

LEWISHAM HIGH STREET, SE13

North end of Lewisham High Street

Rail: *Lewisham or Ladywell (Charing Cross, Waterloo and London Bridge)*
Bus: *75, 89, 181, 185, 208, 261, 278, 284, 484, P4 (Lewisham High Street)*
Open: *Monday-Saturday 9am-5pm*

Hemmed in by chainstores and flanking the Lewisham Centre, this functional market nonetheless appears to be holding its own. Even on a weekday, a steady flow of shoppers cruise the line of stalls stocking up on standard market fare and cheap food. Although unremarkable, the market's jaunty, bulb-lit stalls and friendly atmosphere make it a fun place to stock up on groceries: a number of fruit and veg stalls offer a wide selection, with the remainder selling flowers, fish, eggs, new clothes, watches, household goods, cheap ornaments, underwear, cards, make-up and haberdashery. The fish stall is a particular favourite with its impressive display of everyday fish along with more unusual things like octopus and eel.

Refreshment

Lewisham High Street has several caffs serving standard British food, the most popular being Something Fishy.

Getting a Stall

For further details contact Lewisham Council (see appendix).

southeast

SOUTHWARK PARK ROAD , SE16
(The Blue Market)

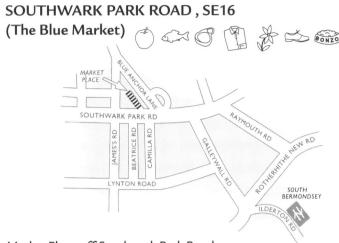

Market Place off Southwark Park Road

Rail: *South Bermondsey*
Bus: *1, 381, P13*
Open: *Monday-Saturday 9.30am-5pm*

Poor old Southwark Park Road. Stuck well below the Thames, lined with squat sixties shoe-box shop units and sandwiched between squalid estates and railway lines, the location doesn't exactly scream hotspot. In the seventies the council made things worse by giving the road over entirely to the relentless south-eastwards bound traffic, side-lining its once-famous street market into a bland precinct. Even now, despite the pretty ash trees and bright municipal benches, the market's slightly artificial setting doesn't seem to help pull in passing trade from the busy High Street – the Sainsburys at Surrey Quays is also leeching the market's customers. The council have attempted to re-brand the market, calling it "The Blue Market" and erecting a sign to advertise the fact. The name derives from Blue Anchor Lane, which is just around the corner.

But it's not all gloom and doom. Although in terms of its range of goods the market isn't exceptional, there is still a bit of atmosphere about the place and most traders seem to welcome banter with regulars.

174

On offer is the normal mixture of things decorative, edible or wearable (Saturdays bring out the most stalls): cheap men's clothes, sports gear, shoes and trainers, nightwear and undies as well as an excellent pet stall. But, as a local market, Southwark Park Road plays to its strengths, the best stalls being those piled high with cheaply priced fruit, veg, eggs, fish, seafood and flowers. The fish stall offers a limited but fresh stock with lots of good deals like small Skate for 90p each and Lemon Soles for £1.30 each.

The friendly fruit and veg man has plenty of regulars popping by for a pound of this or that, and with good reason. Although unremarkable in terms of the trendy or exotic, his produce includes some more uncommon indigenous varieties of fruit bowl mainstays, for example, on the apple front, Katys and Worcesters might also be available as an alternative to Discoveries or Granny Smiths. The plant and flower stall is excellent, with a good selection of bedding plants for just £2.50 a tray, Hardy Cyclmen for £1.50 and pots of healthy looking lavender for just £1; the selection of bulbs is also quite impressive, and at just £1 for 10, tempting for those willing to invest some time in a bit of digging.

southeast

Local Attractions

There is a good butchers in Market Place which helps complement the food offered at the stalls, and there is also a reasonable Sue Ryder shop for those interested in second-hand goods. If you do visit the market, don't miss one of the best charity shops in London, which is just behind The Blue Anchor Pub. It is a courtyard rather than a shop, and is cramed full of interesting second-hand clubber.

Refreshment

If you're looking for somewhere to eat the Pop-In Café just opposite the market on Southwark Park Road is the best place for no-frills British grub. The Blue Anchor Pub is one of the streets landmarks and serves a good pint.

Getting a Stall

For further details contact Southwark Council (see appendix).

WESTMORELAND ROAD, SE17

Westmoreland Street, off the Walworth Road

Tube: Elephant & Castle (Northern, Bakerloo)
Bus: 12, 35, 40, 45, 68, 171, 176, 468, X68 (Walworth Road)
Open: Monday-Saturday 9am-4pm, Sundays 8am-1pm (bric-à-brac)

During the week Westmoreland Road definitely plays second fiddle to East Street market five minutes away, with only a handful of stalls selling fruit and veg, household essentials, cheap clothes and food to the odd passer-by. But on Sundays, the market really comes into its own when it expands to fill the entire length of the road down to Queen's Row as well as a section of Horsley Street with stalls and pitches selling junk and bric-à-brac; by midday the street is buzzing with a chatty mixture of locals from the surrounding estates and visitors from further afield all on the lookout for a serious bargain. And there are plenty to be had amongst the tidal wave of clobber and clothes, much of which is just dumped in piles on the pavement, or spills out of vans, old prams or boxes – the shambolic presentation means prices are very low, so there are plenty of 50p wonders to be had if you are prepared to get stuck in.

176

A lot of the stuff on offer is sub-jumble junk, with broken and dirty casualties from decades past lined up with larger items like fridges, stereos and furniture, but a few stall-holders seem to have weeded out the rubbish and stock attractive and unusual retro knick-knacks and ephemera like cocktail glasses, jewellery, clocks and frames – mostly going for less than a fiver. As with any junk market, shoppers are often sifting through the detritis of other peoples lives and this was very evident at one stall where a large box of family memorabilia including some photo albums and a collection of letters could be picked-up for just a fiver. A fascinating if rather sad bargain.

Household items, such as old cutlery, pans and crockery, are also worth a look, as are the numerous book sections on many of the stalls – amongst the dentist's surgery-style reads are a few more recent titles going for next to nothing, plus the occasional choice buy for fans of period-piece graphics. There used to be some new clothing stalls at the Sunday market, but the clothes are now all second-hand with rails of 50p and £1 items everywhere; although some may throw up the odd find, this is not likely to be the best hunting ground for retro purists. Music, though, is everywhere, with CDs, records and tape stocks including some good bargain. New CDs go for an impressive £6 to £8 for contemporary back catalogue titles on one stall, and in boxes of old albums there is often more on offer than just pop deadwood from the eighties.

Refreshment
The only place to eat on the street is the Westmoreland Café & Burger Bar which is OK for basic grub. For some really good food try the award winning La Luna Pizzeria, which is on Walworth Road, just opposite the market.

Local Attractions
The biggest attraction in this part of town is East Street Market which is just a few minutes walk north and is well worth a visit at the weekends (see page 160 for further details).

Getting a Stall
For further details contact Southwark Council (see appendix).

southeast

177

WOOLWICH & PLUMSTEAD MARKET, SE18

Woolwich Market,
Beresford Square, Woolwich

a) Woolwich Market
b) Plumstead Covered Market

Rail: *Woolwich Arsenal (London Bridge); (or take the ferry south across the Thames from Woolwich North (North London Line)).*
Bus: *51, 96, 99, 244, 291 (Beresford Street)*
Open: *Tuesday, Wednesday, Friday and Saturday 8.30am-5pm, Thursday 8.30am-2pm*

Downstream from the Thames Barrier and easily eclipsed by the more glamorous and intact attractions of near neighbour Greenwich, Woolwich feels like a place nudged just outside the radar of central London's interest. Historically, Woolwich played an essential role in the capital's economy as the home of both the Royal Dockyard and Royal Arsenal, but now those industries have gone (the former in the 1860's, the latter after the Second World War) it seems resigned to being just another slice of inner suburbia.

Woolwich Market (setting up under the Arsenal Gate in Beresford Square since well before the turn of the century), does something to break up the slightly anonymous town centre with a lively range of functional and frivolous goods aimed mainly at the local population.

Essentially operating as a standard provisions market with a contingent of clothes stalls, Woolwich holds few surprises and as such is probably not worth a lengthy trip.

That said, if you live at all locally or just happen to be in the area, the market does offer excellent fruit and vegetables. As you enter the market from the Woolwich New Road, an impressive spread of traditional greens and predominantly British fruits (beansprouts is about as exotic as it gets here) opens out along a triangle of stalls – load up everything for a stew or salad for just a few pounds. The market is very much a focus for Woolwich's many different local communities so the atmosphere is one of good-humoured tolerance. There is also a shellfish stall well-stocked with classic fishy nibbles sold by the cup.

The remainder of the square's stalls are made up of street market standards, household goods and toiletries, shoes, cheap clothes (some stalls might have the occasional bargain amongst the racks of crackling acrylic, but the target audience is definitely teens with firm flesh to bare), carpets, toys and computer games, children's clothes, brand-a-like sportswear, football kits, pet food, hair accessories and jewellery, bags and luggage, bedding and underwear. Stand-out specialisms are the Indian incense and body-art stall, which offers low commitment henna tattoos (the Nike tick icon is popular for £2.99) and cheap burning oils; the man both selling and sewing footballs; and The Music Man, who blasts out Polyfilla tunes of high drama and heartbreak across the market: if your favourite act don't wear cable knits then it's probably best to give his CD stall a wide berth. Woolwich also has great flowers, with a number of stalls offering very tempting prices on both traditional and more exotic blooms, e.g. a large bunch of sunflowers for £1.50. The material and haberdashery stalls also benefit from a bit of competition, with metres of cloth going for as little as £1.

Refreshment

There are a number of friendly greasy spoon cafés round the perimeter of the market, but if you fancy something a bit more substantial, Kenroy's Pie & Eel shop is on Woolwich New Road.

southeast

Plumstead Market
Plumstead Road (see map)

A minute's walk from Woolwich Market is Plumstead Covered Market. The short route between the two sites doesn't promise much: the pavement is flanked with yet more cheap clothes, unbranded trainers and other low-impact bargains. The handful of stalls which make up the market itself occupy just the front section of a grand thirties steel frame warehouse which lies opposite the now defunct Royal Arsenal buildings – the strong sense of departed history makes for a decidedly half-hearted atmosphere. Traders house their goods in attractive beach hut-style cabins, but an apparent lack of interest in presentation means that a lot of stock is just plonked in boxes or on trestles. That said, there are a few specialists tucked away in Plumstead Market whose stalls are model examples of the art of organised cramming: in the far corner, one sells fishing rods and equipment, nearer the front another stocks everything for the keen darts player – from arrows to D.I.Y. trophies.

Second-hand and cheap new clothes, furniture, underwear, material and a rag-bag of bric-à-brac and junk also feature but the best thing about Plumstead Market is the cheap books. Good modern titles, dotted in amongst the saccharine battalions of Mills & Boon, can be found at a number of book sections throughout the market. The Book Browser (the first stall on the far left as you enter) is a small but well-stocked 'proper' book stall, which is particularly strong on older editions of classic fiction and non-fiction (orange and blue Penguins go from £1), and for well-priced and attractive collectables.

Refreshment
The indoor market has the Cabin Café which offers snacks and a reasonable coffee.

Getting a Stall
For further details about a stall at either Woolwich or Plumstead Market contact Greenwich Council (see appendix).

southeast

EAST LONDON

Bethnal Green Road   182
Billingsgate   186
Brick Lane   188
Chrisp Street   195
Columbia Road   197
Kingsland Waste   200
Petticoat Lane   204
Queen's Market   210
Ridley Road   212
Roman Road   216
Spitalfields   220
Walthamstow   224
Well Street   228
Whitechapel   229

east

BETHNAL GREEN ROAD, E2

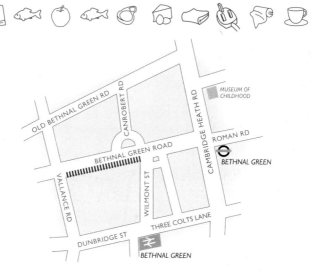

Bethnal Green Road (Vallance Road to Wilmot Street)
Tube: *Bethnal Green (Central Line)*
Bus: *8, D3 (Bethnal Green Road); 106, 253 (Cambridge Heath Road)*
Open: *Monday-Saturday 8.30am-5pm, Thursday 8.30am-12.30pm*

There has been a market on Bethnal Green Road since the 19th century, and despite the arrival of a Tesco store and the neglect of the local council, Bethnal Green Market is still going strong. The market is an expression of the East End's continued vitality and on any weekday you will see old East Enders rubbing shoulders with Asian and African locals, as well as more recent arrivals from eastern Europe. Despite the mix of people and cultures the atmosphere is friendly with plenty of banter and many traders taking the chance for a chat with regulars when things are a little quiet. This must be one of the reasons for the longevity of the market with people preferring to shop on the street and enjoy a chat than to endure the anonymous experience of supermarket shopping.

As a fairly large, well-established market with a solid base of local customers and a string of competing traders, Bethnal Green Road provides a wide range of goods at persuasive prices. Everything you might need, from bedding to plugs, is available and generally of reliable quality. There is nothing particularly out of the ordinary here, but if you're after a relaxed, no frills market then this one should fit the bill.

The fruit and vegetables are cheap and look fresh, but at this market mangetout is given the cold shoulder in favour of less exotic fare such as broad beans. If you're seeking exotic produce look out for the single Afro-Caribbean stall which is usually to be found here. One stall compensated for its lack of foreign veg with six different types of potato – a range that would put most stalls on Berwick Street Market to shame. A few of the street's shops also sell food from period piece premises, evidence that there is enduring support for specialist trade in an area which seems to have avoided the total destruction of its retail traditions by the convenience revolution.

Bethnal Green has a reasonable selection of clothes stalls, with a spectrum of new men's and women's clothing ranging from middle-aged and functional to semi-designer jeans and jackets. Prices are often, to quote one trader's sign, 'Bloody Cheap!', and there are indeed plenty of solid bargains on standard items like sweat tops, leggings and T-shirts. The underwear stalls are particularly good, with M&S remainders going for around half-price, and plenty of nice cotton bras for £3. A number of rummage-style stalls also have super cheap separates or a lucky dip mixture of things like lipsticks, suntan lotion and hair products. The luggage and bags sold on the market are also slightly better looking than the drably functional clobber you get elsewhere.

One of the most established traders on the market offers a vast selection of toiletries and kitchen cleaning materials at very low prices. Among the good deals were a six-pack of toilet rolls for only 80p and two large bottles of bleach for only £1. The stall-holder explained that her grandfather had run a stall on the same site in the 40's and 50's and although the gene had skipped a generation she was happy to be continuing the family tradition. A more recent arrival to the market was the shoe stall, which made up for its lack of history with the quality and cheapness of its stock with colourful kids' sandals for only £6 and adult shoes for only £8.

Refreshment

There are lots of snack bars and cafés along the course of Bethnal Green Market. Café Alba is on the corner of Wilmot Street and serves a cheap all day breakfast. Further along G.Kelly serves pie and mash in a textbook marble and benches interior, while E.Pellici does Italian-cum-greasy spoon breakfasts and lunches. The latter has 'local institution' written all over it: on site since 1900, this tiny café has beautiful Art Deco woodwork, yellowing celebrity photos, genuinely charming staff, good quality comfort food and bags of collective charisma.

east

Local Attractions

The main attraction in this part of town is The Museum of
Childhood which is at the eastern end of Bethnal Green Road, on
Cambridge Heath Road and is a great place to take children of all
ages. Another interesting destination is the newly developed Oxford
House which is on Derbyshire Street just off the market and has two
art galleries and a café, as well as daily fitness classes.

Getting a Stall

For further details contact Tower Hamlets Central Market Office (see
appendix).

east

BILLINGSGATE, E14

North quay of West India Dock, Isle of Dogs
DLR: *West India Quay*
Bus: *D3, D7, D8, 277*
Open: *Tuesday-Saturday 5am-8.30am*

B illingsgate fish market moved to this modern warehouse in
January 1982 from its City location in Lower Thames Street
from where it had been trading for nearly a thousand years.
Billingsgate's new premises lack the grandeur of the old building (which
was designed by Sir Horace Jones) but, given the commercial nature of
the market and the volume of traffic in the City, such a pragmatic move
was inevitable. The new market, although ugly from the outside, still has
a great atmosphere and continues the great tradition of London's fish
trade.

A stone's throw away from Canary Wharf, the market is easy to
find – one dead giveaway are the seagulls which constantly circle above
it, some of whom seem to have grown huge on the fishy titbits so
readily in supply here. The place is busiest between 6.30am and 8am
when most of the commercial buyers are doing business – haggling over
prices and checking the quality of the stock. Some of the traders are
wholesale only, but it's worth asking as many will sell to individual

customers and newcomers are always given a friendly welcome. It's a great place to come with a recipe in mind and hunt down the freshest ingredients possible – just watch out for the forklift trucks operating at the entrance to the market. Among the fifty or so traders you can find every kind of fish imaginable, such as white sturgeon, spotted dogfish and large catfish still wriggling around in their polystyrene boxes. There's also a comprehensive selection of crustaceans and molluscs with anything from deep-water shrimps to live lobsters with their pincers bound to prevent an unwelcome nip.

east

Refreshment
There are two cafés on the premises but they cater largely for the porters and, although you will be made to feel welcome, you will have to tolerate the ever-present aroma of fish. The only alternative in the area is MacDonalds on the mini roundabout approaching the market.

BRICK LANE

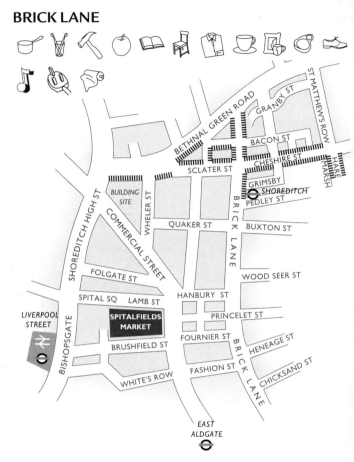

Brick Lane (north of the railway bridge up to Bethnal Green Road), Bethnal Green Road (from Brick Lane to Commercial Street), Cheshire and Sclater Street

Tube: Liverpool Street (Metro & Circle Lines), Aldgate East (District), Old Street (Northern), Shoreditch (East London Line)

Bus: 8 (Bethnal Green Road); 67 (Commercial Street); 25, 253 (Whitechapel Road)

Open: Sunday 6am-1pm

With so many of London's markets being ordered to conform with local government regulations Brick Lane is a last bastion of disorder and lawlessness and all the better for that. Brick Lane becomes the hub of a sprawling disorganised market every Sunday morning. Below are the main parts of the market, but be warned that it changes from week to week so keep your eyes peeled for new streets and archways that have succombed to market fever.

Bethnal Green Road
(from Sclater Street to Commercial Street)
Several years ago Cheshire Street was re-developed and many of the old courtyards that were used for the market gave way to new housing. In 2003 the developers turned their attention to the Commercial Street end of Bethnal Green Road and as a result one of the most ramshackle and interesting parts of the market has been disrupted. Wheeler Street and the archways that led off it have now gone, but the itinerant traders are not easily discouraged and many of them just moved to the northern side of Bethnal Green Road taking with them their odd assortment of second-hand clothes, bric-à-brac, books, CDs and vinyl, cameras and bikes. The chaotic squalor of this part of the market will horrify some, but for hard core bargain hunters it is heaven. I recently found a stylish 70's lamp here for just £2 and a lightweight, top of the range cycle helmet for only £4 (they retail for over £40). The long-term effect of the major development is difficult to predict but whatever changes there are, this spontaneous part of the market seems destined to continue in one way or another.

Sclater Street
The junction with Bethnal Green Road is where an assortment of bric-à-brac stalls and a good value fruit and veg stall congregate. As you proceed down Sclater Street things begin to get a little more organised compared with the chaos of Bethnal Green Road, but there are still several fly-pitches including one regular who sells a reasonable selection of SLR cameras from a blanket on the pavement. Just to the left is the first of Sclater Street's courtyards, this one selling books and used office

east

furniture, with large desks and even computer monitors for around £20. Further along the street are stalls selling new goods including DIY tools and accessories, basic clothing, foodstuffs, and cheap trainers. The lock-ups to the right of the road are worth investigating, one sells crisp cotton sheets for just £2.50 and large white towels for £3.

As you walk down Sclater Street the market opens up to the left to reveal an open square with many of its traders doing business from large trailers. This is the place to see a few of the best sales people in action, using just a microphone and an over-active imagination to generate business. The stall selling electrical goods always has a large crowd, but bargain prices like a portable CD/radio/cassette player for £10 should encourage incredulity – probably better to watch the show rather than risk your money. Among the better stalls in this part of the market is the one selling a huge range of new shoes for £6–£10. Although there's nothing fashionable or stylish about the stock, the stall is always mobbed with locals on the hunt for bargains. The plant stall is also a firm favourite with lots of robust looking potted plants for £2.50–£7. A fairly new arrival is the stationery stall which offers a limited but cheap selection of notebooks, pens and other office essentials. The large meat lorry that used to set up here on a Sunday has gone and in its stead are several stalls offering fresh fruit and veg, olives as well as a fine cheese van. The more healthy selection of food available here is only slightly marred by the hot dog van which fills the air with the smell of burnt onions and cheap meat.

At the far end of this courtyard is Bacon Street which connects with Brick Lane. This street used to be a quiet backwater where dodgy old geezers sold dodgy old goods, but is now a good deal busier with the opening of several new lock-ups selling books, bric-à-brac, furniture and some very cheap kitchenware. Just opposite the square, on the other side of Sclater Street, is another large courtyard selling tools, electrical goods, computer games, kitchen pans and some suspiciously cheap bikes. The fruit and veg stall at the entrance to the courtyard is great value for the basics, and if you can hang around until the end of the day prices drop even further. " come on... I want to go home" exclaims the woman as she holds out large bags of bananas for £1.

east

Cheshire Street (from Brick Lane to Hare Marsh)

Cheshire Street has undergone something of a transformation in recent years and there are now a handful of smart shops on the street including a great vintage outlet at number 3. These new arrivals complement the variety and disorder of the stalls along Cheshire Street, which sell anything from shirts to shoe laces, trousers to Zimmer frames. One of the best stalls is the one selling thousands of books spread along the pavement for only 50p each. Most of the books are rubbish but amid all the dross are one or two gems worth hunting for. There are also a number of good clothing stalls with one selling High Street labels like M&S and River Island for less than a tenner. As well as all the street activity there is also a large concrete warehouse on the right hand side which has about fifty stalls offering second-hand tools, used electronics, clothing, cameras, books, sheets and towels, kitchenware and a great deal more. The atmosphere here is a little dark, but the roof comes in handy on rainy Sundays. Just on the corner of Grimsby Street is Blackman's

Shoe Shop, a Brick Lane institution which stocks cheap and sensible footwear. Further along there's a narrow alley where a few stalls selling interesting junk and second-hand DIY tools ply their trade. On a recent visit a good condition JVC amplifier was going for just £8 and a large doll's house for only £4 was unearthed amid the chaos.

Brick Lane
(from Bethnal Green Road to under the railway arches)

Ironically, Brick Lane is one of the quietest and least interesting parts of Brick Lane Market. The junction with Sclater and Cheshire Street is busy with passing traffic and the few fruit and veg stalls in this area are always buzzing with the stall holders hollering their wares. The north part of Brick Lane has fewer stalls but does have a good clothing stall selling High Street seconds at knock-down prices – trousers, shirts and jumpers for £10 each. The main attraction of this part of the market is the 24-hour beigel bakery which makes the freshest beigels in town.

South of the junction with Sclater and Cheshire Street, there are two large indoor second-hand outlets under the arches on Grimsby Street. One of the lock-ups stocks bikes, furniture, records and bric-à -brac while the other specialises in a huge selection of furniture. Just opposite Grimsby Street, under the railway bridge is a large stall selling second-hand furniture and bric-à -brac. Further along, past Shoreditch tube station, there are a few more junk shops which are a regular feature of the market and usually have things of interest. On a recent visit they had an industrial size floor sander for £150, which was a terrific bargain given that they cost more than that to hire for a weekend. It is at this stage that the market peters out and is replaced by trendy cafés and boutiques. There are currently plans to extend the market further south and to hold occasional fashion sales in the pedestrian walkway opposite the Atlantis Gallery.

Local Attractions

Brick Lane Market has always been a good destination for bargain
shopping with lots of unusual junk shops in the area. The main places
to look for second-hand clobber for the home are the second-hand
lock-ups on Bacon Street and Grimsby Street which are referred to in
the main text. There are lots of fashionable stores springing-up along
Cheshire Street with The Shop at number 3 offering an enticing range
of retro clothing, vintage fabrics, jewellery and ceramics. Beyond
Retro is the biggest and best retro clothing outlet in the area.
Although located at the far end of Cheshire Street it's worth the trek
for the massive selection of clothes, shoes and accessories and
discounted rails.

 If Brick Lane has not exhausted you there are quite a few other
markets within walking distance, including Spitalfields, Columbia
Road and Petticoat Lane all of which are open on a Sunday. For
those in search of culture, The Whitechapel Gallery is about 15
minutes walk south of the market, but as the gallery does not always
have exhibitions it's a good idea to phone (020 7522 7888) before
making a special visit.

east

193

Refreshment

There are lots of places to eat and drink on or around Brick Lane, the most famous place being the Brick Lane Beigel Bakery. The best coffee can be found at the two Coffee @ Brick Lane cafés one of which is at the top end near the beigel shop and the other at the southern end of the market at number 154. If you fancy a Sunday curry, further south on Brick Lane is a huge selection of cheap curry houses, of which Aladdin is one of the best.

Getting a Stall

There are many privately run lock-ups at Brick Lane that will rent space on a Sunday, it's best to have a look around and choose your site. For all other street stalls contact Tower Hamlets Central Market Office (see appendix).

east

coffee@brick lane

154 & 157 Brick Lane
Open daily 7 till 8

CHRISP STREET, E14

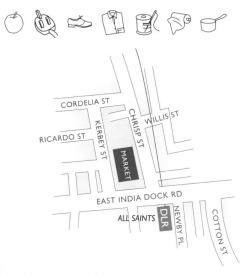

Market Square, Chrisp Street
DLR: *All Saints*
Bus: *D7, D8*
Open: *Monday-Saturday 9.30am-4pm (busiest Saturday)*

This market has been in existence for over a century, pre-dating the rather ugly post-war architecture which now surrounds it. In 1994 the council built a futuristic new roof for the market from metal, concrete and glass, which helps keep the rain off and is about the most attractive structure in the area. Suspended from the roof are large posters showing the market in its Victorian heyday, but far from being a celebration of the market's past, these old photographs only highlight its decline, particularly on a weekday when a mere ten stalls or so set up here.

The best day for a visit to this market is a Saturday when the full complement of stalls offers a reasonable selection of bargain clothing for men, women and children, fruit and veg, fabric and haberdashery, shoes and cheap foodstuffs. Among the stalls worthy of mention was the

195

women's fashion stall with skirts made from contemporary fabric designs for just £7.99, and the shoe stall offering fashionable kids' trainers for just £8 and adult shoes from a tenner. Given the poverty and racial tension in this part of London it was heartening to see the addition of several Asian traders at the market and a fruit and veg stall that stocks a good selection of things like white aloo, long kudo and fresh curry leaves. As well as itinerant traders there are about twenty permanent lock-ups, and it was at one of these that I found some appealing men's shirts for only £4.99. Another interesting trader called themselves Second Tread and specialised in second-hand and slight seconds footwear.

east

Refreshment

There are several good food stalls within the market with the Curry Hut and Wings Chinese Café both offering excellent value. For traditional British grub try Maureen's Cockney Food Bar which is situated a little further back within the shopping complex.

Local Attractions

Despite being so close to the wealth of Canary Wharf, this area has very little to offer the casual tourist. A new Idea Store is planned for the area and this would be very welcome addition to an otherwise barren cultural landscape. For more details about Idea Stores see the review for Roman Road (page 216). Those visiting the market for shopping will find some good food shops with an excellent butchers and fishmongers and Jannah Fabrics for material by the metre. There is also a reasonable charity shop within the market complex.

Getting a Stall

For further details contact Tower Hamlets Central Markets Office (see appendix)

COLUMBIA ROAD, E2

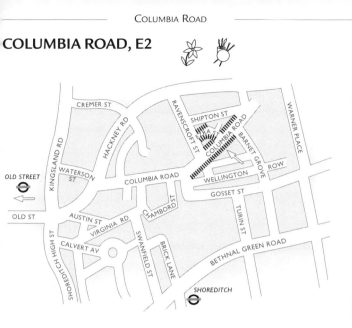

Columbia Road east of Ravenscroft Street to Barnet Grove
Tube: Old Street (Northern), Bethnal Green (Central)
Bus: 26,48, 55
Open: Sunday 8am-1pm

Columbia Road flower market is a real Sunday institution and its appeal seems to extend to those who have no interest in gardening and who just go for the gift shops that run the length of the market and to relax at one of the many coffee shops and eateries that have sprung up around the street. I would recommend approaching the market from Ravenscroft Street and working your way to the eastern end where some of the best cafés are to be found. The market is easy to find from whichever direction you approach it – just walk in the opposite direction to those weighed down with bedding plants, cut flowers and large potted plants. On a busy Sunday morning the streets around the market can often resemble a scene from The Day of the Triffids, with punters making slow progress as they shamble along, obscured by the massive plants they are trying to get home.

197

east

As you approach Ravenscroft Street there are several gift shops catering for the smart crowd that visit here every Sunday. Among the best shops in this part of the market are Pot Luck which sells simple, inexpensive white crockery and The Pot Centre which offers a great range of terra-cotta pots at very competitive prices – huge pots can be bought here for under a fiver. It's a good idea to wait until the end of your visit before buying these bulky bargains –thus avoiding the inconvenience of lugging them around for the duration of your visit.

The stalls selling cheap cut flowers at the junction with Ravenscroft Street mark the start of the market proper, and always have an enticing selection of flowers at well below the prices at your local florist. Here you can get a huge and varied spray for under a tenner and if you don't find what you want look out for the stall at the junction with Ezra Street which has a particularly extensive array of flora, but at slightly higher prices. Although the cut flowers remain a constant, most of the rest of the market varies its stock depending on the season. In the spring it is awash with trays of bedding plants for as little as £3 a tray, and lots of larger plants that will give the urban garden an instant splash of summer colour. As summer turns to autumn evergreens begin to dominate with greenery like lemon-scented goldcrest for £4 a plant (3 plants for £10) and statuesque eucalyptus plants for only £1.50. Large, mature plants can also be found here at well below nursery prices, such as six foot high palms for £15 and orange trees (bearing small fruit) for £20 - the latter reduced to £15 as the market neared its close. Towards Christmas Columbia Road is a great place to come for Christmas trees of all sizes as well as holly, ivy and other festive greenery.

The central avenue of the market is always a scrum with hundreds of people pushing their way along often carrying armfuls of plants. If you get tired of the crush, try weaving between the stalls onto the pavement and taking a look at some of the shops that now line the street. There are lots of good gift, furniture, toy and hat shops to check out and in the middle of the market is the excellent Lee's Sea Food for a fishy treat. Towards the eastern end of the market are some of the best stalls for herbs with healthy looking pots of thyme, rosemary and sage all for £1 or less.

Columbia Road Market is not restricted to Columbia Road, but extends onto Ezra Street and several courtyards connected to it. The main courtyard is just off the junction and has been redeveloped in recent years with several smart shops all of which connect with Columbia Road including Mad Fashion Bitch which sells a great mix of retro clothing and accessories. The courtyard is also home to a new and highly trendy café. Further along there are several more courtyards one of which is dominated by S & B Evans & Sons which offers a huge selection of garden pottery and accessories. The neighbouring courtyard is now given over to second-hand stalls with a pretty reasonable selection of books, clothing and bric-à-brac to sift through.

Refreshment

There are numerous places on and around Columbia Road to get refreshment. Lee's Sea Food sells delicious fried calamari and giant prawns with a wedge of lemon and is highly recommended. Café Columbia also makes good pit-stop if you want to sit down and catch your breath. At the far end of Columbia Road are The Laxeiro Tapas Bar and, further along, The Globe Organic Café which are both safe bets. They have now been joined by a trendy coffee bar called Treacle which serves an expert cappuccino. The Royal Oak is a popular pub and its courtyard on Ezra Street has now been converted into a coffee stall, which rivals the more established coffee shop on the pedestrian walkway a little further along.

Getting a Stall

For further details contact Tower Hamlets Central Markets Office (see appendix)

east

KINGSLAND WASTE, E8

Kingsland Road between Forest and Middleton Road

Rail: Dalston Kingsland
Bus: 67, 149, 242, 243
Open: Saturday 9am-4pm

For six days of the week this part of Kingsland Road is a rather unremarkable row of shops, but on Saturdays it is given over to about forty stalls offering all kinds of new and used goods extending over about a quarter of a mile of wide pavement and parking space. Although there are some smart areas in this part of town, this market does not attempt to cater to the well-heeled and has kept true to its working class origins. If you like your markets clean, tidy and genteel then Kingsland Waste is probably not for you. But for those who enjoy looking for bargains in an authentic and rather seedy East End market it's well worth a visit.

The market is intersected by the busy Richmond Road. It is at this junction heading south that you usually find the carpet man who sells a reasonable selection of carpets and linos at low prices from his van. Continuing south on another stall a dishevelled man was selling an odd assortment of electronic goods, second-hand tools, bike parts, old reference books and a few porn videos. The Marantz tape player looked in reasonable condition and was only £10, but on my return after a wander around the market the man and his stall had gone. From another table a young boy was selling a vast assortment of toy cars with large ones for a £1 and small ones for 50p. It was tempting to imagine this child as a precocious entrepreneur starting out in business, but he was later seen remonstrating with his mum about his pocket money. The nearby stall selling new clothing was good value with some decent quality T-shirts for just £2 and fashionable Nike sports jackets for only £10.

At this part of the market some of the best second-hand stalls can be found with one stall taking-up four tables and offering all kind of used toys, sports equipment, electronic goods, smaller items of furniture and bric-à-brac. It was from here that a small colour TV could be bought for £15, five old fishing rods were only a fiver the lot and a huge Tonka Toy Jeep was just £2. This is a great place to sift through for something unusual. A young woman who was obviously handy with a sewing machine got lucky, finding a box of dress patterns for just a few pounds.

The market is also a very rewarding place to look for new and used equipment. At one of the stalls selling new equipment I found a huge padlock for only £6, which was distressing as I had just spent £25 on a similar lock, and a large Rolson spirit level was a bargain at £6.50.

There are few books to be found on the market these days but there are several stalls offering videos, CDs and DVDs. At one of the better organised stalls an elderly lady offered all kinds of videos from kids' stuff like 'Rosie and Jim' to a selection of Hitchcock classics. As with many of the video stalls on this market, porn figured strongly with something called 'Horny Housewives' taking pride of place. One of the busiest stalls is run by a tall elderly gentleman who displays his selection of paintings, bric-à-brac, tools and collectables with some care and whose stall seems to be a magnet for the locals who visit for a chat and a look at his stock.

east

Further north after Richmond Road there are still more traders, with a greater preponderance of new things for sale although there are one or two second-hand stalls to sift through. The man offering a selection of Clarks shoes in a range of sizes for just £25 a pair is a one of the attractions of this part of the market. The clothing stall at the Forest Road end is also worth having a look at, not everything is top quality but there are always one or two bargains. Recently they had stylish, 100% cotton short sleeved shirts for just a fiver. The stall offering toiletries and household cleaning things was great value with most things for only £1, but you may have to put up with abuse from the staff who seem a rather short tempered bunch.

Kingsland Waste is a great place to visit on a Saturday morning and is a particularly important part of the East End, now that the massive Hackney Wick car boot sale has been closed. The market still appears to be thriving with a core of regular traders and plenty of punters making their way here. The only negative thing to report is the closure of the second-hand shop at nos. 484-486, which complemented the market nicely and is a sad loss.

Refreshment

There is not very much refreshment to be found on the market and a tea and snack van is the only thing on the market itself. The best restaurant in the area is Faulkners at 424 Kingland Road for traditional fish and chips. Kingsland Café is also very popular for an artery clogging fry-up, although it is often difficult to get a seat on market days.

Local Attractions

The Geffrye Museum is about a mile further south along Kingsland Road and is well worth a visit for its unique display of English domestic interiors through the centuries.

Getting a Stall

For further details contact Hackney Council (see appendix).

PETTICOAT LANE, E1

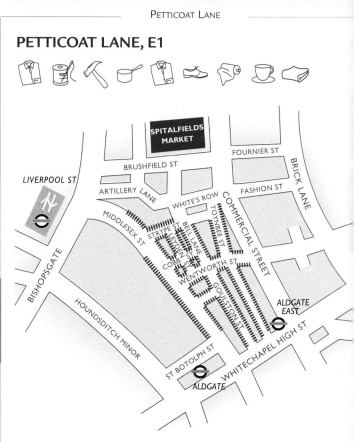

Middlesex Street, Wentworth Street (and adjacent streets)

Tube: Aldgate (Metropolitan, Circle),
Aldgate East (District, Hammersmith & City),
Liverpool Street (Circle, Central, Hammersmith & City, Metropolitan)
Rail: Liverpool Street
Bus: 42, 78, 100 (Houndsditch Minories);
8, 26, 35, 43, 47, 48, 78, 149, 242 (Liverpool Street Station)
Open: All streets Sunday 9am-2pm,
Wentworth Street only Monday-Friday 10am-2.30pm
(shops, fruit and veg and a reduced amount of clothing and general stalls)

204

One of the most confusing aspects of visiting Petticoat Lane Market is the absence of any street by that name. Petticoat Lane was the former name for the main thoroughfare of the market, but it was renamed Middlesex Street in 1830. It is strange that the name of the market has remained in use, but it is appropriate given that the area has always been a place for the sale of clothing. Petticoat Lane is still one of London's most famous street markets, although it is now rivalled by more tourist orientated markets such as Brick Lane and Spitalfields which are both within walking distance.

Despite the competition, Petticoat Lane is still impressively big and busy on a Sunday, when thousands of people flock to the market from Liverpool Street Station to buy a cheap outfit or to just soak up the atmosphere. The streets are lined with hundreds of stalls, concentrating mainly on new clothing, shoes and accessories. Just the sheer amount of people selling shirts or ties is enough to send you into option paralysis. Piles of cheap, cellophaned cotton, acrylic and silk garments seem to be the product of some mass breeding programme, as at each turn more cut-price bargains block your path. Classic price-busting

east

multipacks of knickers, socks and boxer shorts are everywhere, and massive volumes of ladies dresses and separates are also available. Although there's not much outside the purely functional or bandwagon fashion spectrums, there are enough well made and stylish garments to make a trip here worthwhile. On Wentworth Street there was a stall specialising in men's fashion with lots of groovy T-shirts and shirts for just a fiver. On Middlesex Street there was another trader who sold well made and fashionable jeans for just £15 a pair.

At times Petticoat Lane resembles the rag market of Victorian times with stalls selling crumpled nylon clothing in large piles for just £1 an item and an ever changing group of East End's poor sifting through the piles for a bargain. A slightly more organised stall displaying its clothes on rails with everything marked at £3 included a selection of fashionable skirts. The market is also a good place to find leather belts with the stall on Middlesex Street proving the cheapest with leather belts for just £5.

There is more to Petticoat Lane than just clothing however, with quite a few toy stalls selling cheap and tacky plastic stuff for the kids, but one offering plywood models of all kinds for £3-£30. As with everything at Petticoat Lane it's a matter of looking around. There are also numerous bag stalls offering anything from a rucksack to a set of suitcases and all at very low prices. The stall selling large cotton beach towels for just £6 and plain white Egyptian cotton throws for only £20 was also good value. In addition there are also one or two decent shoe stalls offering fashionable and cheap footwear from flip-flops for just a few quid to work boots for around £25. There are also a number of clothing shops in the area which supplement the market, the best known being Benny Dees (Middlesex Street) for cheap bras (around a fiver) and staples like plain T-shirts and leggings.

If you're after a leather jacket visit the undercover area at the Aldgate end of Middlesex Street, known as 'The Designer Market' where you could save serious money on leather jackets and coats. There must be literally hundreds of different styles hanging on the walls, and the amount of individual traders with similar stock means productive haggling is an option.

east

Stand-out specialisms at Petticoat Lane include the international textile shops, which sell everything from African wax prints to Indian sari fabric. At prices starting from around £10 for four yards you can easily afford to do some fairly dramatic curtain-swagging or make yourself a sumptuous dress or skirt. The Middlesex Road end of the market is also a magnet for demonstrators – the people whose job it is to flog us the fragile hope that our lives will be better if we can shred, shine or sharpen something five seconds quicker. Few can resist the power of the patter. Mr Euro-Tool, Mr Shine-Wipe or Mr Borner V-Slicer are performers in the old tradition, so watch, admire and learn. The evangelists at the Bishopsgate end of Middlesex Street might not have such funky props, but the sales message is just as heartfelt: their energetic sing-songs are now a market staple on a Sunday.

Although Sundays is the main day for Petticoat Lane, there is a much smaller weekday market that caters for the locals and offers a few items of clothing along with fruit and veg and other staples. The weekday market is a shadow of the Sunday event and only occupies a small part of Wentworth Street.

Refreshment

Petticoat Lane Market extends down a number of streets, so there are plenty of places to eat as you go round. The Bean is a good café at the Liverpool Street end of Middlesex Street which also has internet access. For traditional British grub without any reference to the super highway, Vernasca's on Wentworth Street is an established favourite. Happy Days on Goulston Street has been offering good quality fish and chips to locals for years and is still going strong. The prawn stall that sells a plate of prawns fried with garlic for just £3, seems to be doing well because now there are three such stalls offering the same very tasty fare.

Getting a Stall

The council are trying to vary the range of the market and are therefore discouraging any more clothing stalls. For further details contact Tower Hamlets Central Market Office (see appendix).

QUEEN'S MARKET, E13

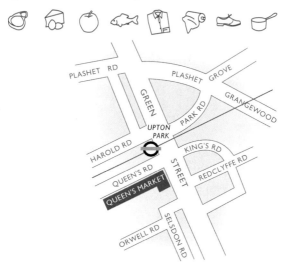

South of Upton Park Station, next to Queen's Road
Tube: Upton Park (Metropolitan, District)
Bus: 58, 104, 330, 376
Open: Tuesday and Thursday-Saturday 9am-5pm

Queen's Market has a long history dating back to Victoria's reign but in the sixties the market was moved to this purpose-built square and in 1979 a low roof was built over it. Twenty years later the place looks squalid and run-down, with little light penetrating beyond the entrance. Despite these badly-planned changes to the market, it is still thriving and even on a wet Monday morning crowds mill around the hundred or so stalls in search of bargains.

One of the reasons this market is still doing well is the large Asian and African communities in Upton Park who still prefer the hustle and bustle of a market to the antiseptic atmosphere of a supermarket. The market is good value for fruit and veg with lots of stalls competing for your custom and bargains like 4 avocados for £1 and bananas for only

15p per lb as well as 5lbs of Desirée potatoes for only 75p. Queen's is also a great place to find Asian and African produce, with many specialist food outlets offering things like Dasheen leaves and bunches of fresh Pak Choi. The handful of fresh fish stalls carry a varied range of catches and are good value with smoked haddock for only £1.49 lb alongside more exotic things like conger eel and octopus. The market also has a profusion of butchers offering all manner of bloody bargains as well as a stall selling farm-fresh eggs.

Queen's Market is also the place for cheap fabric with lots of stalls offering colourful and plain material (including African and Asian designs) with prices starting from £1 per metre. If sewing isn't your thing, there are stalls selling cheap and cheerful clothing, including one specialising in bargain footwear and even one selling tacky plastic watches for only £5.99. Although many of the consumer durables here are of limited appeal, the stall selling large stainless steel pans for £16 is excellent value, as is the discount underwear stall located at the front of the market.

east

Refreshment

For such a large and busy market, Queen's is poorly served for cafés and restaurants. If you do want refreshment, all the eating places are located at the front of the market on Green Street and include Crisp and Crusty Bakers and Queen's Fish Bar. If you fancy some authentic Pakistani food served in a canteen environment at budget prices, head for Mobeen at 222 Green Street.

Local Attractions

Green Street is one of the best places in town to find fabric by the yard. Among the best of these shops is Hardwick Fabrics at number 369, and Hussain Fabrics at number 123 Green Street.

Getting a Stall

For further details contact Newham Council (see appendix).

RIDLEY ROAD, E8

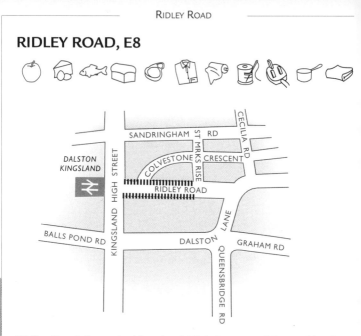

Ridley Road, between Kingsland High Street and St Mark's Rise
Rail: Dalston Kingsland, Hackney Downs
Bus: 67, 149, 242, 243 (Kingsland High Street);
236 (St Mark's Rise)
Open: Monday-Saturday 9am-5pm

R idley Road is one of North London's biggest markets, with attitude to match. Running the length of a street of lock-up shop units between Kingsland High Street and St Mark's Rise, this market is the place where locals from Dalston's diverse communities come to stock up on cheap food and essentials – even on a weekday it's buzzing. The Afro-Caribbean influence in both Dalston and its market is particularly strong, and not only in terms of the massive selection of unusual food products. As the streams of people increase towards midday, the lively – and occasionally slightly abrasive – atmosphere is stoked by shops blasting out reggae and groups of traders and shoppers stopping mid-flow to shoot the breeze.

east

Although Ridley Road is by no means just a food market, the extensive selection of both fresh and preserved produce is probably the magnet drawing most shoppers. Further down towards St Mark's Rise goods become increasingly alien, with tropical standards like mango, cassava and sweet potato joined by baskets and trestles piled with unfamiliar leaves, vegetables, meat and fish, and lurid drinks like 'Sky Juice' on sale by the glass – everyday London seems swallowed up in an atmosphere grafted straight from the Caribbean. The sheer number of rival stalls and shops means you are spoilt for bargains: with each trader offering something at a discount price (like 1lb of garlic for just 60p) you can stock up for a specialist meal for well under a tenner. Staples like lentils, oil, nuts and flour are also extremely cheap, although quantities tend to be large.

In addition, the substantial local Turkish community means that there are plenty of Mediterranean vegetables on offer, with good prices on key ingredients like lemons (10 for £1) and continental parsley (60p a bunch). There is also a huge Turkish food shop on the junction with St Mark's Rise which is ideal for all the other Mediterranean foodstuffs you can't find on the market. More conventional produce is also well-stocked, featuring prices like 6 large oranges for £1 and a large bag of ripe bananas for the same amount. Most street markets these days do not have a fish stall, Ridley Road has several, selling anything from British stalwarts like cod and haddock, to more exotic species like shark and huge conga eels. At one fish stall the crabs were still struggling in vain to escape their fate.

There are a few drawbacks to Ridley Road and one is that it can get very busy, with the narrow gap between stalls clogged with people trying to move in every direction at once. When this happens, traders get a bit shirty if you're not buying courgettes for ten, and might talk you into buying more than you want. Stand firm if you just want a pound of spuds. The squeamish will also find Ridley Road difficult to cope with as it is peppered with stalls selling meat and fish products which bear little resemblance to the innocuous vacuum-packed portions in Tesco's: turkey gizzards, saltfish, goat stomachs, cows' and pigs' feet are all piled up, picked over and chopped up in full view.

east

Food is definitely the thing at Ridley Road, but there are plenty of other goods on offer, with standard market clobber (electricals, cheap and brand-name clothes and shoes, bedding, underwear, cosmetics and hair accessories) dotted throughout, and a smattering of textile units and stalls selling haberdashery and vivid materials like African wax prints, sequined voiles and rainbow selections of satin, cotton and acrylic mixes. One stall dealing in electrical goods had a large selection of boxed, brand-name phones for just £5, while another trader offered a great choice of leather bags and belts for around a fiver. The best clothing stall was at the far end of the market where three shaven headed East Enders sold branded sports and casualwear in large disordered piles. The men made no effort to sell the goods and simply said " seven pounds" to every question asked of them. The clothes were all top quality and new, so the price of £7 an item was a good deal.

Refreshment

Len's Café (half-way down on the left) is secreted underneath the lock-ups for an almost subterranean cup of tea. For something more exotic, try one of the several kebab take-aways that make kebabs good enough to eat when sober. Ridley Bagel Bakery has been re-branded as Mr Bagel, loosing much of its character in the process. At 41 Kingsland High Street, Shanghai serves dim sum throughout the day in a listed interior that used to belong to the area's famous pie and mash shop.

Local Attractions

If you're not too laden with groceries, round the corner in Ashwin Street (off Dalston Lane), there is a big house clearance furniture warehouse which looks like a good bet for finding retro classics in amongst yesterday's clunky oak and pine mediocrities.

Getting a Stall

For further details contact Hackney Council (see appendix).

ROMAN ROAD, E3

Roman Road from St Stephen's Road to Parnell Road

Tube: Mile End (Central, Metropolitan and District)
Bus: 8, D6 (Roman Road); 277, 339 (Grove Road)
Open: Tuesday, Thursday and Saturday 8.30am-5.30pm

Roman Road and its market are a strange mix of the cosmopolitan and the parochial. Approaching the market along Roman Road you will pass a photography gallery, an art gallery, several smart designer clothes shops and even a Buddhist Centre, and yet by the time you reach the market it feels as though you are in the heart of the East End. Most of the people who visit the market are locals and one of the stall-holders spoke of the other side of Victoria Park as though it were some distant and exotic land. Although the market conforms to many of the stereotypes of the East End it is actually a lot cleaner and smarter than commonly assumed and with Victoria Park and the Regent Canal nearby, a place well worth visiting.

216

The market begins at the junction with St Stephen's Road. There was a small indoor market here for some time, but it was never a great success and has now closed. A similar fate has befallen the fabric trader who was a familiar face at the market, but the mysterious stall that sells women's garments one at a time from a box is still going strong. The pitch is always surrounded with eager local women waiting for the next item in the hope that it will be in a style they like and in a size that fits them – price is never a problem as most items are sold for just a few pounds. There are other more conventional clothing stalls along this part of the market offering terrific deals like kids' combat trousers for just £3 and T-shirts for just £2. The jewellery stall near the junction with William Place is also good value with lots of funky silver designs for £5-£75.

Further along there's a stall selling fashionable shoes at around £20 a pair and another dealing in cheap fashion clothing with most items for less than £10. There are also some reasonable underwear stalls with bras for as little as £3 and three pairs of cotton knickers for just a few quid. The stall specialising in fashionable menswear was good value with Peter Werth T-shirts for £5 and sweat shirts for just £10. There's also a good trainer stall at this part of the market and the cheap cosmetics stall is also worth a mention with lipsticks and eyeliners for a pound.

It is at this point in the market, between Libra Road and Hewison Street, that most of the fruit and veg stalls are located. The fruit and veg are good quality but, unlike Ridley Road, there is not much of a cultural mix here, and the food is not very varied as a result. The CD stall makes up for this monotony by playing an eclectic mix of music. On a recent visit shoppers went about their business accompanied by an aria from La Bohème. The busiest stall was the one selling accessories, which was surrounded by women and girls sifting through the hairbands, clips and plastic jewellery – all priced at 20p.

The eastern end of the market is the most interesting for discounted clothing with several stalls specialising in slight seconds and end of line garments from leading designers and High Street chains. The stall on the junction with Usher Road is long established and has hundreds of French Connection seconds for just £3, other less prestigious labels are just £1. Many of the seconds are very slight with a pair of FCUK chinos found here with no discernable fault for the standard £3.

Roman Road Market is still a great place to spend a morning, but there are a few glum faces along the street and more than a dozen empty shops along the market. One trader bemoaned the market's decline and blamed it on a change in public shopping patterns: "...people used to come from all over the place to shop here. Now they want to shop in places like Blue Water." Another trader was less philosophical about the situation, instead resorting to laconic asides to punters. One old geezer gave the man some comfort, "what have you got to complain about, you're young, you like doing-up old cars and of course there's always a bit of the other...mind you, interest in that goes in the end." And with that he was off down Roman Road.

Refreshment

L. Randolfi caff at the western end of the market is very popular, and is close to the Italian pizzeria La Vecchia Napoli. Further along, Franco's Coffee Bar serves a good coffee as does the Café inside the Idea Store on Gladstone Place. For a traditional pie and mash meal try G. Kelly which has two shops on Roman Road.

Local Attractions

The Idea Store situated on Gladeston Place, just off Roman Road, is a fantastic new type of library. It offers CDs, DVDs and internet access as well as books and even has a coffee shop.

Getting a Stall

The market is run by Tower Hamlets Council (see appendix).

east

SPITALFIELDS

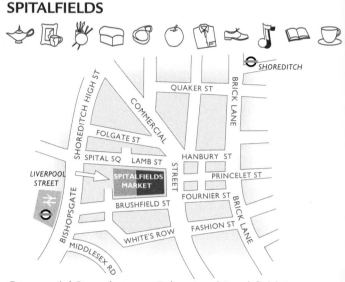

Commercial Street between Folgate and Brushfield Street

Tube: Liverpool Street (Central, Metro & Circle lines)
Bus: 67 (Commercial Street);
8, 26, 35, 43, 47, 48, 78, 149, 242 (Liverpool Street)
Open: Monday-Friday 9am-6pm and weekends (food stalls and shops),
Sunday 11am-3pm (Main Sunday Market)

Spitalfields Market was recently at the centre of a campaign to save about a third of the building from redevelopment. The evident building work and wooden boarding at the Liverpool Street end of the market are testament to the failure of this campaign. The market now occupies about half the space it did before, but still manages to cram in about the same number of stalls, by making them a little smaller and putting them closer together. The reduction in space is regrettable, but it does give the market a more crowded and hectic feel which is actually quite welcome if you like the hustle and bustle of markets like Camden and Portobello. It is also worth noting that the market is still huge – occupying what remains of the large Victorian wrought iron structure that served as a wholesale fruit and veg market until 1991.

east

On a busy Sunday there are several hundred stalls here offering all kinds of things from organic fruit and veg and farm fresh meat to designer wares and bric-à-brac. Most of the food stalls are concentrated at the front of the market which is on Commercial Street, the fruit and veg stalls are large and well stocked with organic produce (for which you pay a premium). There are also several top quality bread stalls and a butcher who sells a limited range of meaty cuts from a caravan in the corner. Not all the stalls in this part of the market are dedicated to food and at one of the entrances is a very good second-hand stall offering unusual things from old angle-poise lamps for a fiver to some large chandeliers that seemed in pretty good nick (see front cover photo-graph). A few other regulars in this part of the market include the salsa and Latin music stall, the trader specialising in unusual men's shirts and coats for anything from £10 to £50 and the small book stall that offers paperbacks for £2 per book.

Further into the market you can track down all kinds of hand-made goods with Spitalfields acquiring a growing reputation for the number of independent artisans that sell their wares here. Among such stalls was one selling handmade bags from original materials for only £28 with purses for only £4, while another offered beautiful and distinctive leather bags for £50. The stall selling hand-made silk bedding was also well worth taking a look at, with a kingsize duvet cover and two pillow cases for £90, and quite a few items reduced to £75. The stall selling unusual Italian designed and manufactured house-hold goods was also very appealing with a set of kids' cutlery in bright colours for £9.99 and a great looking CD box in clear coloured plastic for £19.99. Another stall had a stunning display of new and vintage Danish household goods such as tablecloths, vases and trays - none of which were cheap, but all of which were good quality. The stall offering handmade kids' hats and jumpers for £12 was very tempting for those wanting to dress their little darlings. For adults seeking to clothe them-selves there is plenty to choose from with one stall offering designer trousers for £30 a pair, while another sold good quality T-shirts and sweat shirts with original designs for only £10. One of the most popular clothing stalls stocks second-hand shirts and tops with all garments sold for a fiver. Other second-hand clothing dealers tend to have a more selective stock and higher prices, but even among these

east

traders die-hard bargain hunters can find the odd £1 rail. Consumer durables are all well and good, but my favourite stall in Spitalfields is the German bakery which is at the back of the market and sells a fantastic range of cheesecake and other delicacies – ideal for taking home for a calorific Sunday afternoon tea.

As well as itinerant traders, Spitalfields has many permanent shops. Among the best of these is Bohemia which offers great value retro furniture and lighting and Beedel Coram Antiques which sells antiques and collectables and the largest selection of books to be found in Spitalfields. For new gifts and furniture try 'In...' at the north entrance to the market, which is one the longest established and best stocked gift shops in the area and now offers a selection of larger furniture items.

Refreshment

Spitalfields has over a dozen permanent food stalls and cafés offering good value food from around the world. Among the stalls can be found anything from a Mexican taco to Thai curry. There is also a seating area shared by all the stalls. Among the best places to get a coffee are Spitz which is a large and established coffee bar at the Commercial Street end of the market and The Mediterranean Café which is just a few doors down and is popular with the stall holders. For a coffee on the move, there is a mobile cappuccino van at the far end of the market.

Local Attractions

Three other markets lie within walking distance of Spitalfields – Columbia Road, Brick Lane and Petticoat Lane. An early morning visit to Columbia Road flower market, followed by a rummage for bric-à-brac at Brick Lane and finished off by an afternoon at Spitalfields is a great way to spend a Sunday. Culture vultures might like to visit the Whitechapel Gallery which is about 10 minutes' walk south down Commercial Street on Whitechapel High Street.

Getting a Stall

The popularity of the market has meant that prices are now comparable to Camden or Portobello Market. If you're interested phone Spitalfields Development Group on 020 7247 8556.

east

WALTHAMSTOW, E17

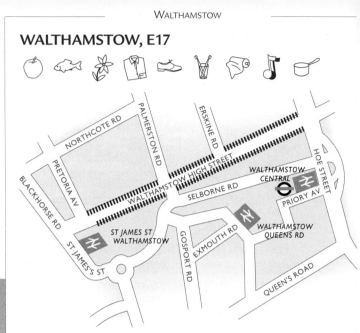

Walthamstow High Street

Tube/Rail: Walthamstow Central (Victoria)
Bus: 20, 48, 58, 69, 97, 230, 257, 275, 357, W15, W19
Open: *Monday-Saturday 9am-5pm*

Many locals claim that this is the longest market in Britain, which is probably an exaggeration given the size of Portobello Market (see page 106), but it is certainly quite a trek from St James Street to the end of the market at Hoe Street. Many local markets are now facing difficulties with the ascension of the supermarket, but Walthamstow is a rare and wonderful exception. There are many reasons for Walthamstow's continued success among them the fact that the wide thoroughfare of Walthamstow High Street has been pedestrianised, making it a natural focal point, as well as a great place for shopping and strolling. The shops in the area complement the market rather than compete with it, with some excellent butchers, fishmongers and continental food shops.

There are about 500 stalls lining the half mile route of the market selling all manner of things. Cheap shoe stalls abound with one of the best situated towards the Hoe Street end of the market selling fashionable women's shoes for between £5 and £25. Another shoe stall offered slight seconds of men's shoes for just a tenner, which included some fashionable suede shoes that appeared in good nick. Although the clothing is not as trendy as that found at Camden market, there are plenty of stalls selling street fashion at keen prices such as the one flogging overstocks and slight seconds from High Street shops like River Island, Monsoon and Evans for £5 a garment. Another trader had simple cotton jackets with the Gap label for only £10, rather than the £40 charged on the High Street. Among the many fabric stalls on the market there's a particularly good one on the junction with Palmerston Road offering quality curtain fabric for as little as £3.99 per metre; and another further along sells Asian and African fabrics at very low prices. Walthamstow is also a good market to visit for kitchenware and household goods with large aluminium pans for just £10 and bargains like 5 bars of soap for £1 and 36 toilet rolls for just £3.99.

There are some superb fruit and veg stalls with one selling carrier bags of seedless grapes for only £1 and another offering 2lb of best vine tomatoes for the same price. Walthamstow used to have a very limited range of fruit and veg, but there has been an increase in diversity in recent years and what you can't find on the market can always be found at other food stores along the route. Likewise, the H. Clare stall has been selling quality fresh fish here for umpteen years, but only the basics, for more exotic fish try the fishmongers opposite.

Unusual stalls at Walthamstow market include the tape and CD stall which offers a massive selection of tapes for just £1 each. Music on tape is becoming a thing of the past, but most people have a cassette player in their car and for a few quid they can find something to add to their in-car music collection. Another quirky feature of the market is Bev's Homemade Cakes which sells colourfully decorated cakes for £2-£2.40, with all cakes guaranteed free from artificial flavourings and small samples for those who want to try before they buy. The market also has two stalls where the name of 'Dyson' is mud, trading as they do in

east

225

Hoover bags and accessories. For romantics who would rather return to their loved one with flowers than vacuum cleaner accessories, there are several stalls selling cut flowers and one dealing in cheap bedding plants. Among the good deals were large pots of heather or brightly coloured coreoposis for just £2 a pot.

Walthamstow High Street is an ideal place to visit if you want to see a neighbourhood market still in its prime. Unlike many local markets it's busy even on a weekday – although Saturday is the best day to go. A good way to approach the market is through the wonderful Springfield Park and Walthamstow Nature Reserve which will take about 45 minutes, but gives you a soothing dose of nature before the hustle and bustle of the market.

east

Refreshment

Among the best places to find good British food on the market is Copperfield Snack Bar (at the top end near Hoe Street), as well as Bunters' Grill and First Stop Café (in the middle part of the market). L.Manze pie and mash shop is an established favourite, while Café Rio is a more recent, but equally popular café with seating outside on fine days. If you don't mind eating on the move there are lots of food stalls on the market including Seth's Spice Hut for Indian snacks and The Old Tea Bag, which despite the name serves a decent cuppa.

Local Attractions

Walthamstow High Street has some interesting shops along its route with many charity shops including the largest Oxfam shop in the capital at the Blackhorse Road end of the market. There is also a great range of fabric shops on the High Street and some excellent food shops which, combined with the market, make this a great place to shop on a weekend.

Getting a Stall

For further details contact Trading Standards Office, 8 Buxton Road Walthamstow E17, Tel: 020 8520 4071.

227

WELL STREET. E9

Well Street from Morning Lane to Valentine Road
Rail: Hackney Downs (Liverpool Street),
Hackney Central (Broad Street)
Bus: *26, 30, 277*
Open: *Monday-Saturday 9.30am-4pm*

T he founder of Tesco supermarket, Jack Cohen, had a stall here over seventy years ago so it's only fitting that the Tesco store at the top end of the market takes most of the local trade today. These days there are only a few if any stalls here during the week and just a handful on Saturdays selling fruit and veg as well as cheap and basic clothing. The quality butchers and excellent bicycle repair shop make this an interesting street, but one not worth venturing too far to visit.

Getting a Stall
For further details contact Hackney Council (see appendix).

east

WHITECHAPEL, E1

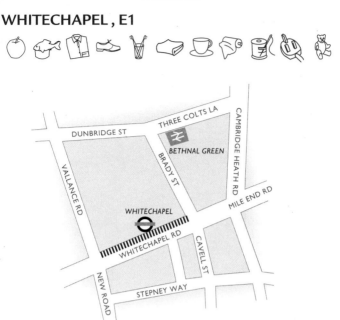

North side of Whitechapel, from Vallance Road to Brady Street

Tube: *Whitechapel (Metropolitan, District)*

Bus: *25, 253*

Open: *Monday-Saturday 8.30am-5.30pm, Thursday 8.30am-1pm*

Whitechapel market has a long history dating back to the 17th century. In Victorian times most of the traders were Irish and Jewish immigrants to the East End. Both communities have now largely left the area and their place has been taken by the Bangladeshi community that has now established itself in Whitechapel. Blooms restaurant at no. 90 was one of the last remaining legacies of the market's Jewish past, but that closed in the mid nineties to make way for a fast-food outlet. The memorial to Edward VII erected by the Jewish community of East London in 1911, which stands opposite the Royal London Hospital, gives some indication of the area's heritage.

east

The market is still a popular place to shop for the local community and there is a reasonable range of goods among the fifty or so stalls that do business here. There are several cheap stalls selling material by the yard, some of which have interesting Asian fabrics. The clothes stalls are pretty mixed with lots of cheap but frumpy garments, but also some excellent fashion items at knock-down prices. Among the recent bargains found here were women's Indian cotton slacks for only £8, and there was also a very busy stall selling hundreds of Top Shop garments for £1 each. The most unusual traders are the two fish men who both have stalls selling huge frozen fish from large freezers placed on the pavement. The fish are packaged and bear names such as Rohn and Bual and do not look appetising for those unfamiliar with them. It might be better to stick to the fresh mackerel and haddock which are also available. Likewise, most of the shoes available are pretty awful, but one stall specialised in trainers and had some reasonable styles for £10 a pair. Other items on offer include small electrical goods, haberdashery, bags, kids' clothes and toys, fruit and veg (both basic and exotic) and a stall selling good value kitchen equipment.

Whitechapel is a thriving local market and its continued success is largely due to the Bangladeshi community from where most of its traders and customers now come. If you want to see London at its most vibrant and multicultural, then Whitechapel Market is definitely a good first stop.

Refreshment

Whitechapel High Street does have a few rather dodgy pubs, but is poorly served for cafés and restuarants. Taja, at the beginning of the market, serves excellent Indian food, and Peckish? is a small sandwich bar at the other end of the market which does a reasonable coffee. For good cheap Indian food it might be better to try some of the places on Brick Lane which is five minutes walk from the market.

Local Attractions

The main cultural landmark in this part of town is the Whitechapel Gallery which is dedicated to modern art and has the added attraction of a great coffee shop. The shops on Whitechapel High Street tend to complement the market with lots of cheap clothing shops and Asian food stores. KVJ is just a few doors down from Whitechapel Gallery and is the cheapest place in town for batteries, blank CDs, ink cartridges, and other essentials.

Getting a Stall

For further details contact Tower Hamlets Council (see appendix).

east

FARMERS' MARKETS

London Farmers' Markets
Webite: www.lfm.org.uk
E-mail: info@lfm.org.uk

Blackheath SE3
Blackheath Rail Station Car Park,
2 Blackheath Village
Rail: Blackheath
Open: Sunday 10am-2pm

Ealing W13
Leeland Road, West Ealing
Transport:
Open: Saturday 9am-1pm

Islington N1
Essex Rd (Opposite Islington Green)
Tube: Angel
Open: Sunday 10am-2pm

Marylebone W1
Cramer Street Car Park,
Corner Moxon Street
(off Marylebone High Street)
Tube: Baker Street
Open: Sunday 10am-2pm

Notting Hill W8
Car Park behind Waterstones
(ccess via Kensington Place)
Tube: Notting Hill
Open: Saturday 9am-1pm

Palmers Green N13
Palmers Green Rail Station Car Park
Tube: Southgate & Wood Green
(then bus)
Open: Sunday 10am-2pm

Peckham SE15
Peckham Square, Peckham High St
Rail: Peckham Rye or Queens Road
Bus: 12, 36, 171, 345
Open: Sunday 9.30am-1.30pm

Pimlico Road SW1
Orange Square, Corner of Pimlico
Road & Ebury Street
Tube: Sloane Square
Bus: 211, 11 & 239
Open:

Swiss Cottage NW3
O2 Centre Car Park,
Finchley Road (near Homebase)
Tube: Swiss Cottage
Bus: 13, 82, 113, 268, 187
Open: Wednesday 10am-4pm

Twickenham TW1
Holly Road Car Park,
Holly Road (off King Street)
Open: Saturday 9am-1pm
Transport:

Whetstone N20
High Street (opposite Waitrose)
Tube: Totteridge & Whetstone
Open: Friday 11am-4pm

Wembley Park SW19
Wimbledon Park First School,
Havana Road
Tube: Wimbledon Park
Open: Saturday 9am-1pm

Farmers' Markets are a relatively new concept in this country, but the number of such markets in the London area has increased rapidly in recent years and this has offered a lifeline to many farmers who were struggling to find a market for their goods. The idea is a simple one, giving farmers the chance to sell their own produce direct to the public at well-run food markets managed by the London Farmers' Markets organisation. The markets are not only good places to stock up on incredibly fresh, high quality, seasonal produce they are also a chance to meet the people that produce the food and understand the passion that many food producers have for their work and the skills they bring to bear in it.

The Farmers' Market in Pimlico is a good example of what you can expect from these events. The market takes place in a small, tree shaded square in one of the smarter parts of Pimlico with a statue of the young Mozart looking down upon the activity that involves about twenty stalls every Saturday morning. There are quite a few stalls offering seasonal vegetables with unusual things like Swiss chard and pumpkin among the more usual British vegetables including a fine selection of root vegetables and some sturdy looking celery stalks – very different from the anaemic examples you find in the supermarket. At one stall a Norfolk farmer was selling honey from his 250 hives for £3.25 a jar and fresh egg, including duck eggs. The farmer was very keen to discuss his farm and was enthusiastic about the markets which have provided a valuable source of income for him, so much so that he now spends the weekend in London and also trades at Blackheath Market on a Sunday.

The Manor Farm stall sells all kinds of food products made from their own livestock including game pies for £4 each and four large venison burgers for a very reasonable £3.50. Another meat stall at the other end of the market was offering even better value with things like six farm produced sausages for £2.50 – comparable with supermarket prices, but of much better quality, and large packs of cooked ham for only £2. The sole cheese stall at the market offered a fantastic selection of their own cheeses, some of which were made using buffalo milk from their own herd. I did want to ask how they milked a half-tonne buffalo,

but resisted the temptation. For the less adventurous they had a well matured cheddar for £1.20 per 100 grams. There are also several fresh fish stalls with things like monkfish for £16 per kilo and wild sea bass for £14 per kilo. Larkins Farm stall offered healthy looking chickens for £8 a bird and a good selection of farm made jams for £2.25 a jar which is again comparable to supermarket prices. The young farmer was very enthusiastic about the market and explained that it was great to meet customers who shared his interest in food. He proudly displayed his new diabetic jam which was specially produced to meet the needs of a particular customer.

One of the best stalls was that run by Chegworth Valley farm which sold a great range of apple juices for £3 per bottle as well as strawberries for £1.50 per punnet and several varieties of apples. In supermarkets you only get generic apple juice at various levels of freshness — at this stall you could choose the juice from different varieties of apple producing different levels of sweetness. The only consistent thing is the freshness of the product. Other stalls included several very good bread and cake stalls, a flower stall with produce from the traders' own market garden and a stall selling lavender and lavender products with strongly scented lavender soap for £5 a bar.

The Pimlico market is typical of the farmers' market experience, although not all the venues have the same charm as this Pimlico square. What all the markets share is good value produce and a belief in properly produced food. Unlike many privately run markets where the traders are usually dissatisfied with how the markets are run, the traders at these markets have nothing but praise for the London Farmers' Markets organisation and the effort they put into promoting the various markets under their control. Visiting a farmers' market is a great experience not only for the great food you can find there, but also for the chance to see that rare thing – British farmers with smiles on their faces. As one trader put it, "...if it wasn't for these farmers' markets I don't know what we would be doing now".

Other Food Markets

This section only covers official farmers' markets run by the organisation London Farmers' Markets. There are other markets which also offer farmers' the opportunity to sell directly to the public, the only difference being that they are not exclusively open to farmers and allow other food traders to sell their wares as well. The best of these markets are Borough Market, Spitalfields Market on a Sunday, Merton Abbey Mills (which has a very good selection of food stalls) and Covent Garden which hosts regular food markets run by renowned food writer Henrietta Green.

Car Boot Sales

Battersea Technology Centre SW8
Battersea Park Road
Every Sunday 1.30pm-5pm
Cars £8, Vans £15
Tel: 07941 383 588

Bounds Green N22
Nightingale School, Bounds Green Rd
Sundays 7am-1pm (6am set up)
Cars £10, Vans £17, 250 pitches
Contact: Red Arrows
Tel: 020 8889 9017

Chiswick W4
Chiswick Community School,
Staveley Road
First Sunday of month (except Jan),
7am-1pm (set up from 7am)
Cars £8, Vans £15, 200 pitches
Tel: 020 8747 0031

Chiswick W4
Southfield Primary School,
Southfields Road
Last Sunday of each month,
10am-2.30pm (March-November)
Cars £5, Vans £10, 100 pitches
Tel: 020 8994 6173

Colney Hatch N10
Skate Attack Field, Opp. Tesco (A406)
Every Sunday 2pm-5pm April-Sept
Cars £10, Vans £20, 350 pitches
Contact: Red Arrows
Tel: 020 8889 9017

Grafton School (Holloway) N7
Grafton School, Bowman's Place,
off Holloway Road (behind McDonalds)
Saturdays 8am-4pm,
Sundays 10am-2.30pm
Cars from £8, 100 pitches
Tel: 01992 717198

Greenford, Middlesex UB6
Ravenor School, Rosedene Avenue
One Saturday per month, 12am-2pm
Cars £8, Vans £10, 100 pitches
Tel: 020 8578 6169

Hayes, Middlesex UB3
Hayes FC, Church Road
Every Wednesday & Friday
8am-2pm (set up 7am)
Cars £15, No Vans, 70 pitches
Tel: 01494 520 513

Hounslow, Middlesex UB3
Hounslow West Station Car Park
Every Saturday & Sunday
7.30am-2pm (set up 7am)
Cars £8, Vans £12, 150 pitches
Contact: Bray Associates
Tel: 01895 639 912 / 637 269

Hounslow, Middlesex UB3
Hounslow Heath Garden Centre,
Staines Road
Sundays & Bank Holidays, 7am-1pm
Cars £8, small trailers £2, small vans
£9, vans £10, vans £15, 250 pitches
Tel: 020 8890 3485

Kilburn NW6
St Augustine's School, Oxford Road
Saturdays 11am-4pm, (set up 8am)
Cars £11, Vans £20
100 pitches
Tel: 020 8442 0082

The Lee Valley Market Site N18
Harbet Road, Edmonton
Every Sunday 6am-1pm
Cars £9, Vans £15
Tel: 01992 638664

Nine Elms SW8
New Covent Garden Market,
Nine Elms Lane
Every Sunday 9am-2pm
Cars £12, Vans £18
Tel: 01895 639 912

Penge and Crystal Palace SE20
St John's School, Maple Road, Penge
Saturdays 9am-3pm (set up 8am)
Cars £10, Vans £12-15
100 pitches
Tel: 020 7263 6010

Portobello Road W11
Under the Westway canopy on
Portobello Road
Every Sunday 9am-4pm (set up 8am)
Cars and vans from £12
200 pitches
Contact: Country Wide
Tel: 01562 777 877

Ruislip, Middlesex UB3
Queensmead Sports Centre,
Victoria Road South
Saturdays 7am-2pm (May-Sept)
Cars £10, Vans £12
300 pitches
Contact: Irene Calver
Tel: 020 8561 4517

Tottenham N17
Tottenham Community Sports Centre,
Tottenham High Road
Thursdays from 7am
Cars £8, Vans £10
40 pitches
Contact: Countryside Promotions
Tel: 01992 468 619
www.countrysidepromotions.co.uk

Tottenham N15
Earlsmead School, Broad Lane
Saturdays 7am-1pm (set up 6am)
Cars £10, Vans £20
150 pitches
Contact: Red Arrows
Tel: 020 8889 9017

Wood Green N22
New River Sports Centre,
White Hart Lane
Fridays from 6am
Cars £9, Vans £11
60 pitches
Contact: Countryside Promotions
Tel: 01992 468 619
www.countrysidepromotions.co.uk

TOP TWELVE LONDON MARKETS
In alphabetical order

1.	Borough Market	150
2.	Brick Lane	188
3.	Camden Market	54
4.	Church Street Market	71
5.	Columbia Road Market	197
6.	Deptford Market	157
7.	East Street Market	160
8.	Greenwich Market	166
9.	Portobello Market	106
10.	Spitalfields Market	220
11.	Swiss Cottage Market	88
12.	Walthamstow Market	224

THE WEEK AT A GLANCE

CENTRAL LONDON	M	T	W	T	F	S	S
Berwick Street & Rupert Street	●	●	●	●	●	●	
Charing Cross Collectors' Fair						▲	
The Courtyard	●	●	●	●	●	●	●
Covent Garden	❶	❹	❹	❹	❹	❹	❹
Earlham Street	●	●	●	●	●	●	
Leadenhall	●	●	●	●	●		
Leather Lane	L	L	L	L	L		
Lower Marsh	L	L	L	L	L	▼	
Piccadilly Market		❶	❹	❹	❹	❹	
Smithfield	✪	✪	✪	✪	✪		
South Bank Book Market	❷	❷	❷	❷	❷	❷	❷
Strutton Ground	L	L	L	L	L		
Tachbrook Street		●	●	●	●	▼	
Whitecross Street	L	L	L	L	L		
NORTH LONDON							
Alfie's Antiques Market			●	●	●	●	●
Bell Street						▲	
Camden				▼	▼	●	●
Camden Passage			❶	❷		❶	▲
Chalton Street					L		
Chapel Market		●	●	●	●	●	●
Church Street		●	●	●	●	●	
Hampstead Community Market						●	●
Hoxton Street	▼	▼	▼	▼	▼	●	
Inverness Street	●	●	●	●	●	●	
Kilburn Square	●	●	●	●	●	●	
Nag's Head	●	●	❶	●	●	●	❸
Queen's Crescent				▲		●	
Swiss Cottage					●	●	●
Wembley Sunday Market							▲
WEST LONDON							
Bayswater Road & Piccadilly						▼	❹
Hammersmith Road	●	●	●	●	●	●	
King's Road Antiques	❶	❶	❶	❶	❶	❶	
North End Road	●	●	●	▲	●	●	
Portobello	▼	▼	▼	▲	●	●	▼
Shepherd's Bush	●	●	●	▲	●	●	

	M	T	W	T	F	S	S
SOUTHWEST LONDON							
Battersea High Street					●	●	
Brixton Market	●	●	●	●	●	●	▼
Broadway and Tooting	●	●	▲	●	●	●	
Hildreth Street	●	●	▲	●	●	●	
Merton Abbey Mills				❶		●	●
Nine Elms Sunday Market							▲
Northcote Road	▼	▼	▲	▼	●	●	
Wimbledon Stadium							▲
SOUTHEAST LONDON							
Bermondsey					✪		
Borough Market					▲	●	
Choumert Road & Rye Lane	●	●	●	●	●	●	
Deptford Market			●	▲	●	●	
East Street		●	●	●	●	●	●
Elephant & Castle	●	●	●	●	●	●	
Greenwich Market				❶	❹	●	●
Lewisham High Street	●	●	●	●	●	●	
Southwark Park Road	●	●	●	●	●	●	
Westmoreland Road	●	●	●	●	●	●	❸
Woolwich & Plumstead Road Market		●	●	▲	●	●	
EAST LONDON							
Bethnal Green Road	●	●	●	▲	●	●	
Billingsgate		✪	✪	✪	✪	✪	
Brick Lane							▲
Chrisp Street	●	●	●	●	●	●	
Columbia Road							▲
Kingsland Waste						●	
Petticoat Lane	▼	▼	▼	▼	▼		▲
Queen's Market		●	●	●	●	●	
Ridley Road	●	●	●	●	●	●	
Roman Road			●		●	●	
Spitalfields	▼	▼	▼	▼	▼	▼	●
Walthamstow	●	●	●	●	●	●	
Well Street	●	●	●	●	●	●	
Whitechapel	●	●	●	▲	●	●	

KEY

●	Open all day	✪	Open early mornings only
▲	Open half-day	❶	Antiques Market
L	Lunch time markets	❷	Book Market
▼	Market partially open	❸	Bric-à-brac
		❹	Arts & Crafts

APPENDIX

Listed below are all the relevant council addresses if you're interested in trading at a council run market:

Camden Council
Environmental Department,
Consumer Protection Services,
Camden Town Hall,
Argyle Street,
WC1H 8NL
Tel: 020 7974 6917

Greenwich Council
Public Services,
11th Floor Riverside House,
Woolwich High Street,
SE18 6DN
Tel: 020 8921 5835

London Borough of Hackney
Environment Directorate,
Dorothy Hodgkin House,
12 Reading Lane,
E8 1HJ
Tel: 020 8356 3367

London Borough of
Hammersmith and Fulham
Environmental Protection Division,
Town Hall Extension,
5th Floor,
King Street,
W6 9JU
Tel: 020 8753 1081

Islington Council
Public Protection Department,
159 Upper Street,
N1 1RE
Tel: 020 7527 3830

Kensington and Chelsea Council
Market Office,
72 Tavistock Road,
W11 1AN
Tel: 020 7727 7684

Lambeth Council
Market Trading,
53 Brixton Station Road,
SW9 8PQ
Tel: 020 7926 2530

Lewisham Council
Wearside Service Centre,
Wearside Road, Lewisham,
SE13 7EZ
Tel: 020 8314 2050

Newham Council
Property & Design Department,
City Gate House,
246-50 Romford Road, Forrest Gate,
E7 9HZ
Tel: 020 8472 1450 ext 32964

Southwark Council
Markets Department,
SAST House,
Dawes Street,
SE17 1EL
Tel: 020 7525 6000

Tower Hamlets
Market Service,
29 Commercial Street,
E1 6BD
Tel: 020 7 377 8963

Wandsworth Council
Markets Department,
Room 59, Town Hall,
Wandsworth High Street,
SW18 2PU
Tel: 020 8871 6381

Westminster City Council
Licensing Department,
33 Chester Street,
SW1X 7XD
Tel: 020 7641 7822

Other useful addresses for
insurance and display equipment:

The National Market Trader's
Federation
Hampton House, Hawshaw Lane,
Hoyland, Barnsley, South Yorkshire,
S74 0HA
Tel: 01226 7490 211

Shopfittings Direct
Unit 3 Colonial Way, Watford,
WD24 4PR
Tel: 01923 232425

INDEX

Asian / Afro-Caribbean Food
Bethnal Green Road   p.182
Borough Market   p.150
Brixton Market   p.122
Broadway and Tooting   p.127 & 129
Choumert Road   p.154
Chrisp Street   p.195
East Street   p.160
Hildreth Street   p.130
Kilburn Square   p.82
Portobello   p.106
Queen's Market   p.210
Ridley Road   p.212
Rye Lane   p.156
Shepherd's Bush   p.116
Whitechapel   p.229

Antiques & Art
Alfie's Antiques Market   p.48
Bayswater Road & Piccadilly   p.96
Bermondsey   p.146
Camden   p.54
Camden Passage   p.62
Church Street   p.71
Columbia Road   p.197
Covent Garden   p.14
Hampstead Community Market   p.75
Greenwich Market   p.166
King's Road Antiques   p.101
Merton Abbey Mills   p.132
Piccadilly Market   p.30
Portobello   p.106

Bags, Belts, Purses and Leatherwear
Bethnal Green Road   p.182
Brick Lane   p.188
Brixton Market   p.122
Camden   p.54
Chalton Street   p.66
Chapel Market   p.69
Church Street   p.71
Courtyard, The   p.12
Covent Garden   p.14
Deptford Market   p.157
East Street   p.160
Greenwich Market   p.166
Leather Lane   p.22
Northcote Road   p.138
Petticoat Lane   p.204
Piccadilly Market   p.30

Portobello   p.106
Queen's Crescent   p.86
Ridley Road   p.212
Rupert Street   p.6
Shepherd's Bush   p.116
Spitalfields   p.220
Strutton Ground   p.39
Whitechapel   p.229
Whitecross Street   p.44
Woolwich Market   p.178

Bedding, Linen & Towels
Bethnal Green Road   p.182
Brixton Market   p.122
Camden   p.54
Chalton Street   p.66
Chapel Market   p.69
Church Street   p.71
East Street   p.160
Greenwich Market   p.166
Hoxton Street   p.77
Kilburn Square   p.82
Leather Lane   p.22
Lower Marsh   p.26
Nine Elms Sunday Market   p.136
Petticoat Lane   p.204
Queen's Crescent   p.86
Ridley Road   p.212
Rye Lane   p.156
Tachbrook Street   p.42
Wembley Sunday Market   p.92
Whitechapel   p.229
Whitecross Street   p.44
Wimbledon Stadium   p.142
Woolwich Market   p.178

Bikes
Brick Lane   p.188

Books
Alfie's Antiques Market   p.48
Bell Street   p.51
Brick Lane   p.188
Camden Passage   p.62
Greenwich Market   p.166
King's Road Antiques   p.101
Kingsland Waste   p.200
Merton Abbey Mills   p.132
Piccadilly Market   p.30
Plumstead Road   p.178
Portobello   p.106
South Bank Book Market   p.36

Bric-à-brac

Alfie's Antiques Market   p.48
Bell Street   p.51
Brick Lane   p.188
Camden Passage   p.62
Deptford Market   p.157
Greenwich Market   p.166
Hampstead Community Market   p.75
Kingsland Waste   p.200
Nag's Head   p.84
Piccadilly Market   p.30
Portobello   p.106
Swiss Cottage   p.88
Westmoreland Road   p.176

CDs/Tapes

Berwick Street & Rupert Street   p.6
Brixton Market   p.122
Camden   p.54
East Street   p.160
Greenwich Market   p.166
Hoxton Street   p.77
Kingsland Waste   p.200
Lower Marsh   p.26
Nine Elms Sunday Market   p.136
Portobello   p.106
Roman Road   p.216
Rye Lane   p.156
Shepherd's Bush   p.116
Spitalfields   p.220
Strutton Ground   p.39
Swiss Cottage   p.88
Walthamstow   p.224
Wembley Sunday Market   p.92
Westmoreland Road   p.176
Whitecross Street   p.44
Woolwich & Plumstead Road   p.178

Childrenswear

Brixton Market   p.122
Broadway   p.127
Chapel Market   p.69
Chrisp Street   p.195
Church Street   p.71
Greenwich Market   p.166
Kilburn Square   p.82
Merton Abbey Mills   p.132
Roman Road   p.216
Spitalfields   p.220
Swiss Cottage   p.88
Woolwich Market   p.178
Whitechapel   p.229

Clothes (New)

Battersea High Street   p.120
Bethnal Green Road   p.182
Brick Lane   p.188
Brixton Market   p.122
Camden   p.54
Chapel Market   p.69
Church Street   p.71
Earlham Street   p.18
East Street   p.160
Elephant & Castle   p.164
Greenwich Market   p.166
Hoxton Street   p.77
Kilburn Square   p.82
Leather Lane   p.22
Lewisham High Street   p.173
Merton Abbey Mills   p.132
Nine Elms Sunday Market   p.136
Northcote Road   p.138
Petticoat Lane   p.204
Portobello   p.106
Queen's Crescent   p.86
Ridley Road   p.212
Roman Road   p.216
Southwark Park Road   p.174
Spitalfields   p.220
Wembley Sunday Market   p.92
Westmoreland Road   p.176
Whitechapel   p.229
Woolwich & Plumstead Road   p.178

Clothes (Second-hand)

Bell Street   p.51
Brick Lane   p.188
Brixton Market   p.122
Camden   p.54
Elephant & Castle   p.164
Greenwich Market   p.166
Kingsland Waste   p.200
Lower Marsh   p.26
Nag's Head   p.84
Northcote Road   p.138
Plumstead Road Market   p.178
Portobello   p.106
Spitalfields   p.220
Westmoreland Road   p.176

Crafts

Bayswater Road & Piccadilly   p.96
Brixton Market   p.122
Camden   p.54
Covent Garden   p.14
Greenwich Market   p.166
Lower Marsh   p.26
Merton Abbey Mills   p.132
Piccadilly Market   p.30
Portobello   p.106
Spitalfields   p.220

Delicatessen / Organic Food

Battersea High Street   p.120
Borough Market   p.150
Chapel Market   p.69
Farmers' Markets   p.232-236
Greenwich Market   p.166
Leather Lane   p.22
Merton Abbey Mills   p.132
Northcote Road   p.138
Portobello   p.106
Spitalfields   p.220

Electrical Goods

Berwick Street & Rupert Street   p.6
Brick Lane   p.188
Brixton Market   p.122
Chapel Market   p.69
Church Street   p.71
Deptford Market   p.157
East Street   p.160
Lower Marsh   p.26
North End Road   p.103
Portobello   p.106
Queen's Crescent   p.86
Ridley Road   p.212
Whitechapel   p.229
Wimbledon Stadium   p.142

Fabrics & Haberdashers

Berwick Street & Rupert Street   p.6
Brixton Market   p.122
Broadway   p.127
Camden   p.54
Chalton Street   p.66
Chapel Market   p.69
Chrisp Street   p.195
Church Street   p.71
East Street   p.160
Kilburn Square   p.82
Leather Lane   p.22

Lewisham High Street   p.173
Lower Marsh   p.26
Nag's Head   p.84
Petticoat Lane   p.204
Portobello   p.106
Queen's Market   p.210
Ridley Road   p.212
Roman Road   p.216
Shepherd's Bush   p.116
Walthamstow   p.224
Whitechapel   p.229
Woolwich Market   p.178

Fish

Berwick Street & Rupert Street   p.6
Billingsgate   p.186
Borough Market   p.150
Brixton Market   p.122
Broadway and Tooting   p.127 & 129
Choumert Road   p.154
Church Street   p.71
Deptford Market   p.157
Hoxton Street   p.77
Kilburn Square   p.82
Leadenhall   p.20
Lewisham High Street   p.173
Merton Abbey Mills   p.132
Nag's Head   p.84
North End Road   p.103
Queen's Crescent   p.86
Queen's Market   p.210
Ridley Road   p.212
Shepherd's Bush   p.116
Southwark Park Road   p.174
Walthamstow   p.224
Whitechapel   p.229
Woolwich Market   p.178

Flowers and Plants

Battersea High Street   p.120
Berwick Street   p.6
Brixton Market   p.122
Camden Passage   p.62
Chapel Market   p.69
Church Street   p.71
Columbia Road   p.197
East Street   p.160
Earlham Street   p.18
Hammersmith Road   p.99
Hildreth Street   p.130
Inverness Street   p.80
Kilburn Square   p.82

Lewisham High Street   p.173
Lower Marsh   p.26
Merton Abbey Mills   p.132
North End Road   p.103
Northcote Road   p.138
Portobello   p.106
Queen's Crescent   p.86
Southwark Park Road   p.174
Strutton Ground   p.39
Tachbrook Street   p.42
Walthamstow   p.224
Woolwich Market   p.178

Fruit and Vegetables
Battersea High Street   p.120
Berwick Street   p.6
Borough Market   p.150
Brick Lane   p.188
Brixton Market   p.122
Chapel Market   p.69
Farmers' markets   p.232-236
Inverness Street   p.80
North End Road   p.103
Northcote Road   p.138
Portobello   p.106
Spitalfields   p.220
Walthamstow   p.224
Whitechapel   p.229

Furniture
Alfie's Antiques Market   p.48
Bermondsey   p.146
Brixton Market   p.122
Camden   p.54
Camden Passage   p.62
Deptford Market   p.157
Greenwich Market   p.166
Plumstead Road Market   p.178
Portobello   p.106
Ridley Road   p.212
Spitalfields   p.220
Tachbrook Street   p.42
Tooting   p.229

Haberdashery
Broadway   p.127
Chapel Market   p.69
Chrisp Street   p.195
East Street   p.160
Kilburn Square   p.82
Lewisham High Street   p.173
Lower Marsh   p.26

Ridley Road   p.212
Whitechapel   p.229
Woolwich Market   p.178

Household / Kitchenware / Toiletries
Battersea High Street   p.120
Berwick Street   p.6
Bethnal Green Road   p.182
Brixton Market   p.122
Broadway   p.127
Chalton Street   p.66
Chapel Market   p.69
Church Street   p.71
Deptford Market   p.157
East Street   p.160
Elephant & Castle   p.164
Hoxton Street   p.77
Kilburn Square   p.82
Kingsland Waste   p.200
Leather Lane   p.22
Lower Marsh   p.26
Nag's Head   p.84
Nine Elms Sunday Market   p.136
Portobello   p.106
Queen's Crescent   p.86
Rye Lane   p.156
Shepherd's Bush   p.116
Spitalfields   p.220
Walthamstow   p.224
Westmoreland Road   p.176
Whitechapel   p.229
Whitecross Street   p.44
Wimbledon Stadium   p.142
Woolwich Market   p.178

Jewellery and Watches
Alfie's Antiques Market   p.48
Bayswater Road & Piccadilly   p.96
Bermondsey   p.146
Brixton Market   p.122
Broadway   p.127
Camden   p.54
Camden Passage   p.62
Church Street   p.71
Covent Garden   p.14
Deptford Market   p.157
East Street   p.160
Elephant & Castle   p.164
Greenwich Market   p.166
Kilburn Square   p.82
Leather Lane   p.22
Lewisham High Street   p.173

Lower Marsh   p.26
Merton Abbey Mills   p.132
Northcote Road   p.138
Piccadilly Market   p.30
Portobello   p.106
Queen's Crescent   p.86
Roman Road   p.216
Spitalfields   p.220
Strutton Ground   p.39
Swiss Cottage   p.88
Tachbrook Street   p.42
Woolwich Market   p.178

Meat
Battersea High Street   p.120
Borough Market   p.150
Brixton Market   p.122
Broadway and Tooting   p.127 & 129
Camden Passage   p.62
Chapel Market   p.69
Covent Garden   p.14
East Street   p.160
Farmers' Markets   p.232-236
Greenwich Market   p.166
Leadenhall   p.20
Merton Abbey Mills   p.132
Queen's Crescent   p.86
Ridley Road   p.212
Smithfield   p.34
Spitalfields   p.220
Wembley Sunday Market   p.92

Shoes
Bethnal Green Road   p.182
Brick Lane   p.188
Brixton Market   p.122
Chalton Street   p.66
Chapel Market   p.69
Chrisp Street   p.195
Church Street   p.71
Deptford Market   p.157
East Street   p.160
Hoxton Street   p.77
Leather Lane   p.22
Lower Marsh   p.26
Nag's Head   p.84
Nine Elms Sunday Market   p.136
Petticoat Lane   p.204
Ridley Road   p.212
Roman Road   p.216
Rye Lane   p.156
Shepherd's Bush   p.116
Southwark Park Road   p.174

Spitalfields   p.220
Strutton Ground   p.39
Walthamstow   p.224
Wembley Sunday Market   p.92
Whitechapel   p.229
Whitecross Street   p.44
Woolwich Market   p.178

Tools and Hardware
Brick Lane   p.188
Chapel Market   p.69
Greenwich Market   p.166
Kingsland Waste   p.200
Nine Elms Sunday Market   p.136
Petticoat Lane   p.204
Rye Lane   p.156
Wembley Sunday Market   p.92
Whitecross Street   p.44

Toys
Camden   p.54
Chalton Street   p.66
Church Street   p.71
Covent Garden   p.14
East Street   p.160
Elephant & Castle   p.164
Greenwich Market   p.166
Hoxton Street   p.77
Kilburn Square   p.82
Lower Marsh   p.26
Nine Elms Sunday Market   p.136
Northcote Road   p.138
Petticoat Lane   p.204
Swiss Cottage   p.88
Wembley Sunday Market   p.92
Whitechapel   p.229
Whitecross Street   p.44
Woolwich Market   p.178

Videos/DVDs
Berwick Street   p.6
Brixton Market   p.122
Deptford Market   p.157
Hoxton Street   p.77
Kingsland Waste   p.200
Leather Lane   p.22
Strutton Ground   p.39
Swiss Cottage   p.88
Whitecross Street   p.44
Wimbledon Stadium   p.142

the end